EXTENSION
WORK

CHRISTINE FLINN

MEREHURST

This book is dedicated to my cousin Margaret for creating my initial interest in cake decoration;
to my tutors at the College of Art and Technology, Newcastle upon Tyne – Jean Bogan, Ken Henderson and
A. G. Binns; and, last but not least, to my husband Chris and daughter Amy.
My thanks to Jill Hargreaves, Helen Johnson and Graham Tann for their help;
to J. D. Smith (3 Deacons Close, Croft, Warrington, Cheshire WA3 3EN) for the vertical cake holder;
to E. T. Webb (18 Meadow Close, Woodley, Stockport, Cheshire SK6 1QZ) for the cake dummies;
to Perfectionery (3a Alcock Street, Runcorn, Cheshire WA7 1NA) for the wedding cake stand;
to Jane Alford for her cross stitch alphabet and rose design for the Cross Stitch Birthday Cake on page 43;
and to Patchwork Cutters (3 Raines Close, Greasby, Wirral L49 2QB).

First published in 1996 by Merehurst Limited, Ferry House, 51–57 Lacy Road, Putney, London SW15 1PR

Copyright © Merehurst Limited 1996

ISBN 1 85391 577 7

Edited by Helen Southall
Designed by Jo Tapper
Photography by Graham Tann
Colour separation by Pixel Tech., Singapore
Printed by Wing King Tong, Hong Kong

Acknowledgements
The publisher would like to thank the following for their assistance:
Anniversary House (Cake Dec.) Ltd., Unit 5, Roundways, Elliott Road, Bournemouth,
BH11 8JJ, Tel: 01202590222; Cake Art Ltd., Venture Way, Crown Estate, Priorswood,
Taunton, TA2 8DE, Tel: 01823 321532; Guy, Paul & Co. Ltd., Unit B4, Foundry Way, Little End Road,
Eaton Socon, Cambridge PE19 3JH, Tel: 01480 472545; Squires Kitchen, Squires House, 3 Waverley Lane,
Farnham, Surrey, GU9 8BB, Tel: 01252 711749.

NOTES ON USING THE RECIPES

For all recipes, quantities are given in metric, Imperial and cup
measurements. Follow one set of measures only as they are not
interchangeable. Standard 5ml teaspoons (tsp) and 15ml tablespoons
(tbsp) are used. Australian readers, whose tablespoons measure 20ml,
should adjust quantities accordingly. All spoon measures are assumed to
be level unless otherwise stated.
Eggs are a standard size 3 (medium) unless otherwise stated.

CONTENTS

INTRODUCTION

*W*hen I started cake decorating, a celebration cake was usually decorated with royal icing, and sugarpaste was only used for slab cakes. The main form of decoration was run-out sugar pieces coupled with line work. This is probably why I enjoy piping so much. I hope the following pages portray my love of the craft, and will inspire you to experiment with the techniques illustrated. The first cake with extension work that inspired me was by Geraldine Randlesome (Canada) at the 1st British Sugarcraft Guild National Exhibition in 1985.

For the greatest sense of achievement, try to design your own cake, using the standard techniques, but without copying someone else's design. However, there is no such thing as an original idea, as most designs are inspired by the objects around us. For example, the square format extension work on the cake on page 58 was inspired by the air vents at the gym I use!

This book is organized by degree of difficulty, starting with basic extension work and finishing with competition standard techniques. Working drawings are included, which can be used in conjunction with the step-by-step photographs to make the written instructions easy to follow. The techniques covered include bridged extension work, looped extension work, bridged extension work with draped extension lines, fun extension work with flower paste bridges, crochet work, bridgeless extension work with the use of a cake tin, extension work in conjunction with run-out sugar pieces, and square format extension work.

Even if you have never tried piping before, I hope you will be motivated to have a go at some of the designs in this book. It is not hard to pipe a line as long as you remember the basic instructions: *TOUCH TO START, APPLY THE PRESSURE, LIFT, EASE THE PRESSURE OFF AND DOWN.*

To help my students I teach them a little tune (see below) to go with these instructions. It makes it all so simple!

TOUCH TO START. APPLY THE PRESSURE. LIFT. EASE THE PRESSURE OFF AND DOWN.

BASIC TECHNIQUES & RECIPES

PIPING

All the piping in this book has been done with standard royal icing – normal strength (made with Meri White), which is my personal preference. If you wish to make traditional royal icing from fresh egg white or pure albumen powder, then this would be suitable. You can also choose whether or not to add liquid glucose, gum tragacanth, acetic acid, etc., to your royal icing. For piping purposes, however, royal icing should not contain glycerine (glycerol), which absorbs moisture. Remember this when colouring royal icing and use liquid colours, as some paste food colours contain glycerine.

EXPERT ADVICE

≈

The size of piping bag and consistency of icing should always be in proportion to the size of the piping tube (tip) used, i.e. the smaller the piping tube, the smaller the piping bag and the softer the icing should be.

Never fill a piping bag more than half full with icing as an over-full bag will create more stress on the muscle of your hand and will probably burst or leak.

Do not work with the same bag of royal icing for more than 30 minutes as the icing will dry in the bag and become harder to pipe.

When piping extension lines, it is easier if the cake is at eye level.

BRIDGE WORK

royal icing (without glycerine/glycerol)
EQUIPMENT
scriber
no. 0 or no. 1 piping tube (tip)
fine paintbrush

There is no set rule as to which size of piping tube (tip) a bridge should be piped with; it is personal preference. Some pipe the first line of a bridge with a no. 2 tube, followed by three lines with a no. 1 tube, then three lines with a no. 0 tube. My preference is to pipe the whole bridge with the same tube – either eight lines with a no. 1 tube or fourteen lines with a no. 0 tube.

● Make a paper template and scribe the pattern on to the cake side(s). Pipe the first line of the bridge, then wait at least 20 minutes before piping the next line. (If you leave less than 20 minutes between each line of bridge piping, you run the risk of the bridge collapsing.) Try to ensure that each line touches the previous one without any gaps, because gaps result in a weak bridge which will look untidy and will probably break when the extension lines are piped. When viewed from the side, the bridge should appear to be only the thickness of the line piped. As you pipe, make sure the bridge is not sloping up or down; correct with a paintbrush if necessary.

● Some people recommend brushing the whole bridge with run sugar to fill in any gaps, thereby creating a stronger bridge, but by doing this the object of piping with a fine piping tube is defeated, as the resulting bridge is thick. Moreover, the real skill of bridge work is in being able to pipe a bridge without the need to fill in any gaps.

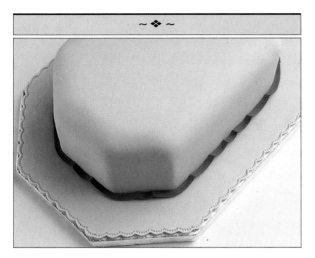

~ ❖ ~

BRIDGE WORK *For a strong, neat bridge, ensure that each line of bridge work touches the previous one without any gaps. As you pipe, make sure the bridge is straight and not sloping up or down.*

RUN-OUT SUGAR PIECES

❖

royal icing (without glycerine/glycerol)
EQUIPMENT
butchers' wrap (acetate)
piece of perspex
masking tape
no. 0 piping tube (tip)
fine paintbrush

◉ Attach a piece of butchers' wrap to the perspex with masking tape. Make a paper pattern for the run-out piece you are making (such as the teddy bear, right). Slide the pattern between the perspex and the butchers' wrap.

◉ Using royal icing, pipe the outline of the piece with a no. 0 piping tube on to the butchers' wrap. Remove the paper pattern from beneath the butchers' wrap. Let down a small amount of royal icing to run sugar consistency and flood the piece, flat rather than domed, using a fine paintbrush to ensure that the run sugar gets into all areas.

◉ Place the piece under an angled desk lamp for approximately 30 minutes to dry the surface of the run sugar quickly and so keep the sheen. Transfer to a warm environment and leave to dry. All run-out pieces, no matter what size, should be completely dry within 24 hours; if the pieces have not dried, the royal icing was not of the right consistency and/or the drying environment was too cold.

DOUBLE-SIDED RUN-OUT PIECES Once the run-out piece is dry, turn it over. Re-pipe all the internal lines, if required, with a no. 0 piping tube, remembering that on the reverse side the lines will be in different positions (see the example of the run-out bear). There is no need to pipe the outline. Flood with run sugar, then dry as for the front of the piece.

Run-out bear (see page 55 for actual size)

A SIMPLE WAY TO WRITE AN INSCRIPTION ON SUGARPASTE

❖

royal icing (without glycerine/glycerol)
sugarpaste
EQUIPMENT
tracing paper
piece of perspex
masking tape
nos. 0 and 1 piping tubes (tips)

● Write or trace the inscription in the chosen style and correct size on a piece of tracing paper. Turn the tracing paper over and attach it to a piece of perspex with masking tape.

● Place the piece of perspex on a work surface, ensuring the tracing paper is against the work surface and the perspex is on top. Pipe the inscription on to the perspex with royal icing using a no. 0 or no. 1 piping tube (tip). Leave to dry for no less than 30 minutes.

● Cover the cake with sugarpaste. Invert the piece of perspex and place it on top of the covered cake so the inscription is in the correct position. Press firmly on the perspex with the palm of your hand, then remove the perspex, leaving an impression of the inscription on the cake. This technique is only suitable for freshly covered cakes.

● Leave the sugarpaste to skin over for 24 hours, then pipe the inscription, using royal icing the same colour as the cake and a no. 1 piping tube. Over-pipe with a different colour and a no. 0 piping tube.

CHAMFERED CAKE BOARDS

❖

A chamfered cake board is made by attaching a small cake board (for example, a 20cm/8 in round board) on top of a larger board (for example, a 25cm/10 in round board). Make sure the smaller cake board is central, and leave

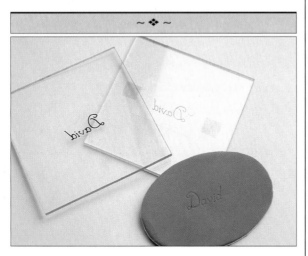

INSCRIBING SUGARPASTE This simple method avoids piping freehand on to the cake's surface. It is also effective used for plaques, as long as the covering medium is soft.

CHAMFERED CAKE BOARDS Fill the difference in width between the two boards with marzipan (almond paste), sugarpaste or royal icing. Make sure the slope is at an even angle all round.

to set in position, if necessary. Pack the difference in width between the two boards with marzipan (almond paste), sugarpaste or royal icing (see picture, left). Once the packing has set, cover with sugarpaste or coat with royal icing. If coating in royal icing, it is easier to coat the top and sloping sides separately rather than both at the same time.

MEXICAN PASTE
❖

250g (8oz/1½ cups) icing (confectioners') sugar
3 tsp gum tragacanth
1 tsp liquid glucose
6 tsp cold water

◉ Sift the icing sugar and gum tragacanth together into a bowl. Add the remaining ingredients and knead well.
◉ Seal in an airtight bag and leave for 24 hours before using.

ROCK SUGAR
❖

125ml (4fl oz/½ cup) water
500g (1lb/2 cups) granulated sugar
60g (2oz/½ cup) freshly made royal icing,
coloured light brown
EQUIPMENT
cardboard box (roughly 20cm/8 in square),
lined with wax paper

◉ Place the water and sugar in a saucepan. Heat gently until the sugar has dissolved, then bring rapidly to the boil until a temperature of 130°C (265°F) is reached.
◉ Remove the pan from the heat and add the coloured royal icing, stirring quickly until it is well mixed (the mixture will start to froth as

ROCK SUGAR *When broken up, rock sugar can be used for a variety of decorative purposes on formal as well as novelty cakes. See the Road Bridge Birthday Cake on page 26.*

soon as the royal icing is added). Pour into the prepared cardboard box and leave to cool.
◉ Once cool, remove the rock sugar from the box and break it up into small pieces with your fingers.

EXPERT ADVICE
≈

Store mexican paste in a sealed, airtight container or bag in a cool place, but not in the refrigerator. If stored in the refrigerator, it has a tendency to break down and become unworkable.

RETIREMENT CAKE

20cm (8 in) stretched octagonal cake
sugarpaste
selection of liquid and paste food colourings
royal icing (without glycerine/glycerol)
apricot, brown and tangerine dusting powders
(petal dust/blossom tint)
piping gel (neutral)
EQUIPMENT
28cm (11 in) stretched octagonal cake board
crimper (optional)
nos. 0 and 1 piping tubes (tips)
fine paintbrush
small cake board (approximately 15cm/6 in)
rice paper
mapping pins
small pieces of sponge
tweezers
stamen cotton

Cover the cake and cake board with sugarpaste. Mark the inscription on top of the cake, as described on page 8, and crimp around the edge of the sugarpaste on the cake board, if desired. Leave to skin over for 24 hours.

Create a paper pattern for positioning the bridge and extension work. Secure the paper pattern to the cake and scribe the outline on to the cake sides. Remove the paper.

Pipe a snail's trail border around the base of the cake with a no. 1 piping tube. Pipe the bridge in dark brown royal icing, referring to the instructions on page 6, if necessary. Pipe the extension lines in royal icing (the same colour as the cake) with a no. 0 piping tube, as shown in step 1 on page 12. The lines should be as close together as possible without touching. Pipe each extension line beyond the bridge and remove the surplus icing with a damp paintbrush. Do not stop on the bridge, as the contact of the piping tube with the bridge could cause the bridge to come away from the cake side.

Once the extension lines are complete, pipe an alternating snail's trail around the top edge of the extension lines with a no. 0 piping tube. Pipe one more line of bridge work in the same colour as the extension lines with a no. 0 piping tube. Pipe in the inscription as described on page 8, if desired.

Trace the butterfly pattern on page 12 on to a piece of paper, and place the paper on top of the small cake board. Place a piece of rice paper (smooth side up) on top of the paper pattern and secure with mapping pins. Create the colours for painting by mixing dusting powder with piping gel and a little water.

Paint over the butterfly pattern lines on the rice paper in brown, then paint in all the areas with appropriate colours, and leave to dry for approximately 24 hours. The rice paper will stretch and ripple when wet (this is why it is pinned down) but it will dry taut.

Cut out the butterfly wings, being careful not to leave fingerprints. Pipe a fat line (approximately 1.5cm/¾ in long) of brown royal icing on the cake top using a no. 1 piping tube. Using tweezers, carefully position the tips of the lower wings into the icing body, propping them at the correct angle with small pieces of sponge. Position the top wings, propping them at a slightly greater angle.

Cut the stamen cotton in half, curve gently and insert into the body to create the antennae. (Inserting the stamen cottons renders the whole butterfly inedible.) Leave to dry, removing the small pieces of sponge after 15 minutes.

EXTENSION WORK *Pipe lines as close together as possible without allowing them to touch. Pipe each line beyond the bridge; do not stop on the bridge as this could cause the bridge to come away from the cake side.*

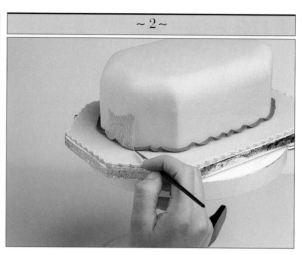

After piping each line beyond the bridge, remove excess icing with a damp paintbrush, maintaining a straight line along the bridge.

BUTTERFLY *Paint the lines of the butterfly in brown, then colour in the different areas. The wet rice paper will stretch and ripple, so make sure it is pinned down carefully. On the cake top, the wings are positioned in royal icing, and propped up with sponge until dry.*

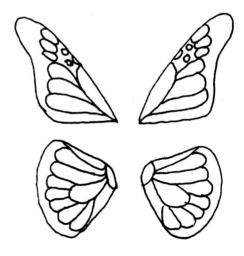

Rice paper butterfly wings

Retirement Cake
working drawing
(enlarge to 142% on
a photocopier)

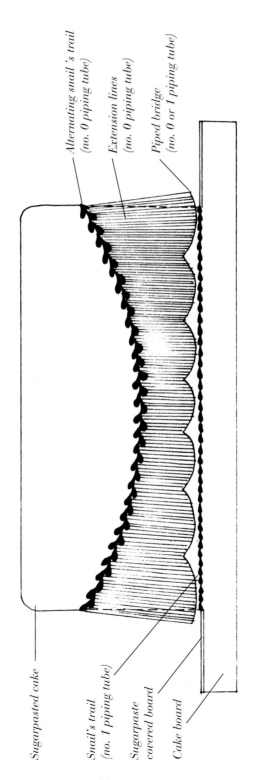

Alternating snail's trail
(no. 0 piping tube)

Extension lines
(no. 0 piping tube)

Piped bridge
(no. 0 or 1 piping tube)

Sugarpasted cake

Snail's trail
(no. 1 piping tube)

Sugarpaste
covered board

Cake board

SINGLE-TIER WEDDING CAKE

royal icing (without glycerine/glycerol)
20cm (8 in) oval cake
sugarpaste

EQUIPMENT

15cm (6 in) square of perspex
masking tape
butchers' wrap (acetate)
nos. 0 and 1 piping tubes (tips)
chamfered cake board (25cm/10 in on 30cm/
12 in board), see page 8
embosser (optional)
posy pick
approximately 100 miniature roses and
125 leaves
tweezers
tilting turntable

● Create a paper tracing from the lace top piece design on page 16 and attach it to a piece of perspex or glass with masking tape. Cover the pattern with a piece of butchers' wrap and attach it to the perspex with masking tape.

● Using royal icing and a no. 0 piping tube, pipe over the pattern, ensuring that all piped lines touch each other to create strength. Over-pipe the main, thicker outlines on the pattern with a no. 0 piping tube, and pipe small bulbs around the edge to secure the piped lines, ensuring that the bulbs touch each other. Leave to dry.

● Cover the cake and chamfered cake board with sugarpaste. Emboss the edge of the cake board, if desired. Leave to skin over for 24 hours. Scribe a faint line around the side of the cake at the height from which you wish the extension work to start. Pressure pipe embroidery in ivory royal icing on the side of the cake, just above the scribed line, with a no. 0 piping tube (see step 1 on page 16). Pressure pipe in ivory royal icing over the embossed decoration around the sugarpaste-covered board (see step 2).

● Release the lace piece from the butchers' wrap, and place on top of the cake, ensuring that it is central. Secure to the cake top with small dots of royal icing (see page 16). Insert a posy pick into the cake top at the top of the lace piece.

● Make a garland of flowers and leaves for the base of the cake, arranging the flowers with tweezers, and reserving some flowers for the top posy. Attach to the cake. Place the cake on a tilting turntable set at no more than a 15° angle. Working at the lowest point on the tilting turntable, begin piping the looped extension work with a no. 0 piping tube. Pipe no more than three loops before turning the cake. Leave at least 15 minutes before piping the next row of loops, from the centre of each loop on the previous row (see step 1 on page 17). Continue piping the loops until the required depth is achieved (see step 2).

● Create a small spray of flowers and leaves for the top of the cake and place in the posy pick.

~ 1 ~

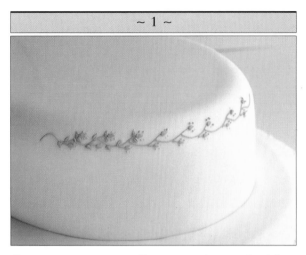

PRESSURE PIPING *Pressure pipe embroidery around the top of the cake. For clarity, icing coloured with 'old gold' colouring has been used here, but the icing should be the same colour as the sugarpaste.*

~ 2 ~

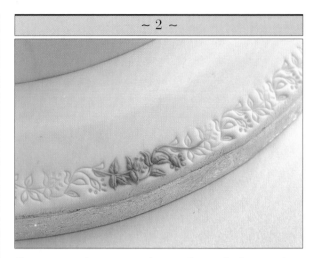

Pressure pipe over the embossed decoration, shown here in gold, around the edge of the chamfered cake board.

~ ❖ ~

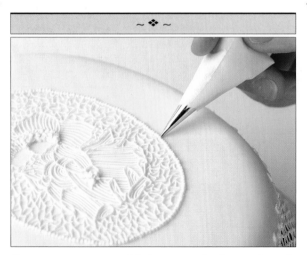

LACE TOP PIECE *Make sure the lace piece is central, then pipe about six small dots of royal icing around the edge to secure it to the cake top.*

Lace top piece (no. 0 piping tube)
(enlarge to 118% on a photocopier)

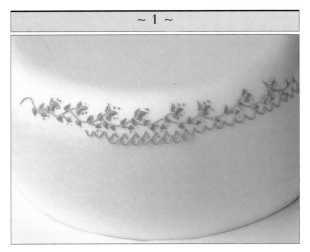

~ 1 ~

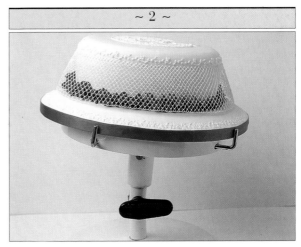

~ 2 ~

EXTENSION WORK *Pipe a row of small loops along the scribed line around the cake using a no. 0 piping tube (tip). Pipe no more than three loops before turning the cake. Leave to dry for 15 minutes before piping the next row, piping from the centre of each loop in the previous row.*

Continue the looped extension work until the required depth is achieved. The work should be done with the cake on a tilting turntable at an angle of approximately 15°, as shown.

Detail of cake top

Single-tier Wedding Cake working drawing
(enlarge to 182% on a photocopier)

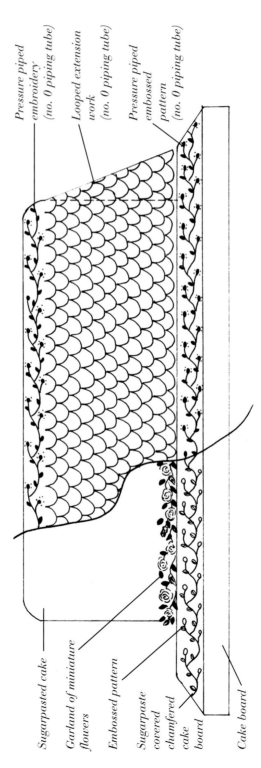

Pressure piped embroidery (no. 0 piping tube)

Looped extension work (no. 0 piping tube)

Pressure piped embossed pattern (no. 0 piping tube)

Sugarpasted cake

Garland of miniature flowers

Embossed pattern

Sugarpaste covered chamfered cake board

Cake board

CHRISTENING CAKE

flower paste
selection of liquid and paste food colourings
20cm (8 in) oval cake, covered with marzipan
(almond paste)
sugarpaste
royal icing (without glycerine/glycerol)
EQUIPMENT
fine metal comb
plastic cake dowels
teddy bear embosser (FMM)
28cm (11 in) oval cake board
embosser (optional)
masking tape
nos. 0 and 1 piping tubes (tips)
15cm (6 in) square of perspex
butchers' wrap (acetate)
small pieces of sponge
tweezers
fine paintbrush

● First make the edible ribbon. Soften and colour some flower paste in the usual way, and roll it out until 1.5mm (¹⁄₁₆ in) thick. Mark and cut into strips 3mm (⅛ in) wide. Indent the top and bottom edge of each strip with a fine metal comb (see step 1 on page 22). Cut the strips into 1.5cm (¾ in) lengths, and drape over plastic (not wooden) cake dowels. Leave for approximately 2 hours, and then remove the semi-dried strips from the dowels. Leave the edible ribbon to dry completely for 24 hours. (See step 2.)

● For edible bows, cut more strips of flower paste, mark with a comb as described above, and shape into bows as shown on page 22. Leave to dry for 24 hours.

● For the teddy bears, soften and colour some flower paste in the usual way, and roll it out until 3mm (⅛ in) thick. Emboss eight teddy bears, and leave, uncovered, for 5–10 minutes. Carefully cut out the teddy bears and transfer them to a piece of sponge. Leave to dry for 24 hours. (See page 22.)

● Cover the cake and board with sugarpaste and emboss the board, if desired. To make a paper template for the cake side design, wrap a strip of paper around the cake, overlapping by 1cm (½ in) where the ends meet. Turn back the extra 1cm (½ in) and fold the strip of paper into eight equal portions.

● Using the working drawing on page 24 as a guide, draw the design on the template and cut it out. Place the paper pattern around the cake, open out the extra 1cm (½ in) and secure with tape. Scribe both the top and bottom edges of the pattern on to the cake side. Remove the paper template.

● Carefully insert the edible ribbon pieces 5mm (¼ in) above the top scribed line all around the cake. No glue is necessary, but this must be done before the sugarpaste cake covering has skinned over. Pipe a snail's trail around the base of the cake with a no. 1 piping tube.

● For the top lattice design, make a tracing of the baby and teddy illustration on page 24, omitting or changing the name as required. Colour it according to the key on page 24. (The pattern needs to be in colour as it will not be possible to see the symbols once the lattice has been piped.) Try to use colours that are easily distinguishable.

● Attach the coloured pattern to a piece of perspex or glass with masking tape (a cake board is not suitable as most are slightly warped). Cover the pattern with a piece of butchers' wrap and attach to the perspex with masking tape. Pipe the lattice on to the butchers' wrap with royal icing and a no. 0 piping tube. First pipe the vertical lines, then the horizontal (see step 1 on page 23).

Create the picture by piping dots with a no. 0 tube into the squares created by the lattice lines in the appropriate colours. If different shades of the same colour are required, start with the darkest shade first, then add an equal quantity of white royal icing to make a lighter shade.

Pipe small bulbs around the edge of the lattice to secure, ensuring that the bulbs touch each other. Leave to dry.

Release the lattice from the butchers' wrap. Place five small pieces of sponge (1.5cm/¾ in square) on top of the cake. Place the piped lattice on top of the small pieces of sponge, ensuring that the lattice is central on the cake top and that the small pieces of sponge protrude beyond the piped lattice.

Using royal icing and a no. 0 piping tube, pipe lines from the cake top up to the lattice ensuring that the lines are straight and not sloping. Continue to pipe lines all around the lattice, keeping them as close together as possible without touching (see step 2). As each small piece of sponge is approached, remove it carefully with tweezers. Leave eight evenly spaced gaps in the extension work (approximately 1.5cm/¾ in wide) for the curtains.

To pipe the curtains, pipe two lines from the lattice edge (in the centre of each gap), one to the middle of the first extension line on the left and the other to the middle of the first extension line on the right, allowing the lines to sag. Continue to pipe lines until the space is filled, all the lines finishing at the same point,

i.e. the middle of the first extension line on either side. (See step 3.)

To complete the curtains, pipe two sloping lines, one from the middle of the first extension line on the left and the other from the middle of the first extension line on the right, to the cake top (approximately 5mm/¼ in in from the extension lines). Keep the lines taut. Continue to pipe lines until the space is filled, all the lines starting at the same point, i.e. the middle of the first extension line on either side. Pipe bows on to the curtains with pink royal icing using a no. 0 piping tube.

Following the lower scribed line, pipe the bridge in pink royal icing around the base of the cake, referring to the instructions on page 6, if necessary. Pipe or paint the eyes, mouth, etc., on to the flower paste bears and attach the bears to the side of the cake with royal icing.

Pipe extension lines in white royal icing using a no. 0 piping tube from the top scribed line to the bridge. The lines should be as close together as possible without touching. Always pipe the lines beyond the bridge and remove the surplus with a damp paintbrush. Never stop on the piped bridge as this could cause the bridge to come away from the cake side.

Leave gaps of approximately 3cm (1¼ in) in the extension work where the bears are attached to the cake. Pipe curtains as before, and pipe pink bows on the curtains using a no. 0 piping tube. Pipe another line of bridge work in white royal icing using a no. 0 piping tube to finish the bridge. Attach flower paste bows to the cake side above each teddy bear.

EDIBLE RIBBON Roll out some pink flower paste until 1.5mm (¹⁄₁₆ in) thick. Mark and cut into strips 2.5mm (⅛ in) wide. Use a fine metal comb to mark dots lengthways along the edges of each strip.

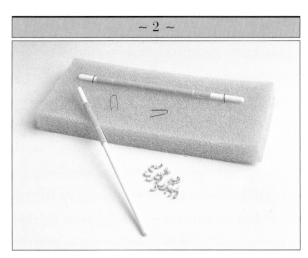

Cut the strips into 1.5cm (¾ in) lengths. Secure plastic cake dowels to sponge with wire, and drape pieces of paste ribbon over the dowels. Leave for approximately 2 hours, then remove the semi-dried pieces and leave for 24 hours to dry completely.

EDIBLE BOWS Cut more strips of pink flower paste, indent with a comb, as before, and make into bows as shown. You will need to make eight bows altogether. Leave to dry.

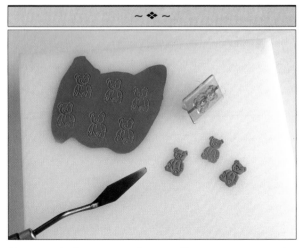

BEARS Soften some brown flower paste in the usual way, and roll it out to 3mm (⅛ in) thick. Emboss eight bears and leave, uncovered, for 5–10 minutes. Carefully cut out the bears, transfer to a piece of sponge, and leave to dry for 24 hours.

FLOATING LATTICE Pipe the lattice in royal icing using a no. 0 piping tube (tip). Pipe the vertical lines first, then the horizontal.

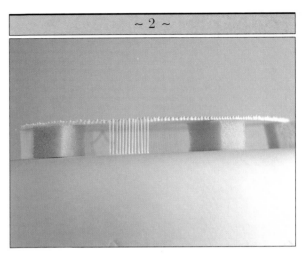

Pipe vertical lines from the cake top up to the lattice edge, ensuring the lines are straight and close together. Remove the pieces of sponge with tweezers as you come to them. Leave eight evenly spaced gaps in the extension work (approximately 1.5cm/¾ in wide).

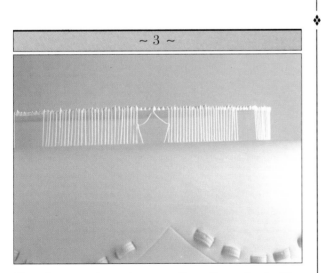

For the curtains, pipe two lines from the lattice edge (in the centre of each gap), one to the middle of the extension line on each side, allowing the lines to sag. Continue piping lines, all finishing in the middle of the first extension line on each side, to fill in.

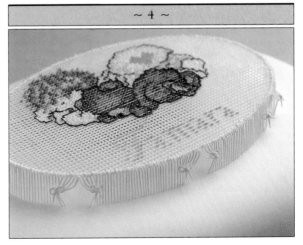

To complete the curtains, pipe two sloping lines, one from the middle of the first extension line on each side to the cake top (approximately 5mm/¼ in in from the extension lines), keeping the lines taut. Pipe more lines to fill in. Pipe pink bows on the curtains.

Christening Cake piped lattice top (actual size)

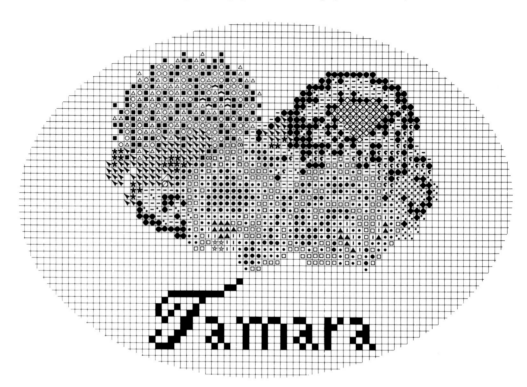

KEY TO COLOURS

⊠	Dark tan	◕	Pink
◎	Tan	⊟	Light pink
▣	Light tan	◈	Ultra light pink
△	Very light tan	⊡	White
◤	Ultra light tan	✫	Black
▱	Coral	▢	Very dark brown
⊘	Light coral	⊡	Dark brown
✹	Flesh	●	Brown
◤	Light flesh	▮	Light brown
◇	Very dark pink	▲	Ultra light brown
⊂	Dark pink	■	Lettering colour

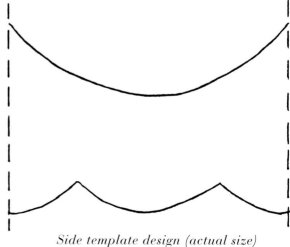

Side template design (actual size)

Christening Cake
working drawing
(enlarge to 173% on a
photocopier)

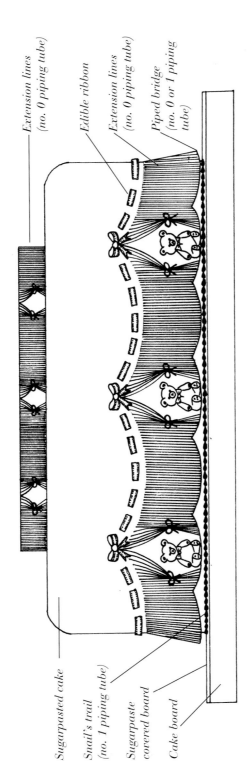

Extension lines (no. 0 piping tube)

Edible ribbon

Extension lines (no. 0 piping tube)

Piped bridge (no. 0 or 1 piping tube)

Sugarpasted cake

Snail's trail (no. 1 piping tube)

Sugarpaste covered board

Cake board

ROAD BRIDGE BIRTHDAY CAKE

20cm (8 in) square cake, covered with
marzipan (almond paste)
blue sugarpaste
mexican paste, see page 9
liquid and paste food colourings
white vegetable fat (shortening)
royal icing (without glycerine/glycerol)
white dusting powder (petal dust/blossom tint)
piping gel (neutral)
flower paste
egg white or gum glue
rock sugar, see page 9

EQUIPMENT

33cm (13 in) square cake board
car patchwork cutter
nos. 0 and 1 piping tubes (tips)
fine paintbrush
piece of perspex
butchers' wrap (acetate)
masking tape
cocktail stick (toothpick)

● Cover the cake and board in blue sugarpaste. Gently press the patchwork cutter on to the top of the cake (see step 1 on page 30), and mark an inscription on the top of the cake, as described on page 8, if desired. Leave to skin over for 24 hours.

● Roll out some red, black and light grey mexican paste until 1.5mm (1/16 in) thick. Lightly grease the cutting edge of the patchwork cutter with white vegetable fat, and cut out one complete car in each colour. The cutter should be regreased after each cut. Moisten the embossed outline of the car with water, and cut out and attach the appropriate coloured pieces of mexican paste (see step 2). Extra pieces may be added to create a 3D effect. Surround the car with dark grey mexican paste.

● Pipe over the impression of the inscription on the cake with a no. 1 piping tube, and over-pipe using a no. 0 piping tube (see page 8). (See step 3.) Paint the clouds on the side of the cake. Create the paint by mixing a small amount of white dusting powder with piping gel and a little water.

● To make the road bridges, cover a piece of perspex with a piece of butchers' wrap and secure with masking tape. Soften the flower paste in the usual way and colour if desired. Roll out the flower paste until 3mm (1/8 in) thick, and transfer to the sheet of perspex. Make a template from the outline on page 29, and cut out eight bridge towers. Roll out the flower paste until 1.5mm (1/16 in) thick, and transfer to the perspex. Make another template and cut out the road sections (eight small pieces plus four of the larger pieces). Allow all the pieces to dry overnight. (See step 1 on page 28.)

● Once the items are dry, glue the pieces together with flower paste glue which is made by mixing a small amount of flower paste with egg white or gum glue until it resembles well-chewed chewing-gum. Use a cocktail stick to apply small amounts of glue to the bridge sections before sticking. Leave to dry. Roll out some dark grey flower paste until 1.5mm (1/16 in) thick, and cut out a strip 1cm (1/2 in) wide. Attach to the bridge with egg white or gum glue. Leave to dry. (See steps 2 and 3.) Reserve the trimmings of dark grey flower paste for completing the road around the corners of the cake.

● To begin the piping on the bridges, pipe a loop on one side only, from one tower to the

other, using royal icing and a no. 1 piping tube, ensuring that the base of the loop is no less than 1cm (½ in) from the road section beneath. Pipe a loop at each end, from the tower to the road, again on one side of the bridge only. Repeat on all four bridges, then leave to dry for no less than 30 minutes. (See step 4.)

● Pipe vertical lines in pairs, using royal icing and a no. 0 piping tube, leaving a larger space between each pair. Ensure that the lines are vertical and not sloping (see step 5). Remove excess royal icing with a damp paintbrush. Once all the vertical lines are complete, pipe a horizontal line across the vertical lines just above the road section. Secure the bridges to the cake board with royal icing, making sure the piping is on the inside. The bridges should be close to the cake's sides, but should not touch them.

● Attach pieces of rock sugar to the corners of the cake and cake board with royal icing. Roll out the remaining dark grey flower paste until 1.5mm (¹⁄₁₆ in) thick, and cut out strips 1cm (½ in) wide. Complete the road around the cake by attaching strips of grey flower paste to the rock sugar with royal icing.

● Complete the extension work on the outsides of the bridges. Flood the remainder of the cake board with piping gel. (Piping gel does not dry; it just skins over.)

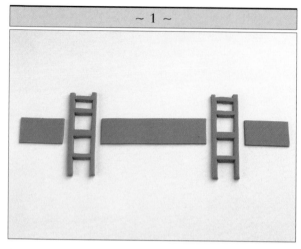

~ 1 ~

ROAD BRIDGES Roll out flower paste until 3mm (⅛ in) thick and cut out eight bridge towers. Roll out more flower paste until 1.5mm (¹⁄₁₆ in) thick, and cut out the road sections (eight small and four large). Leave to dry overnight.

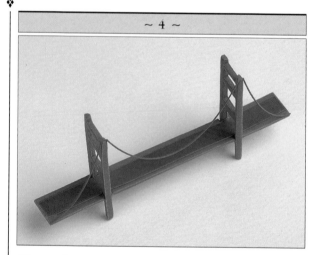

~ 4 ~

Pipe a loop on one side only, from one tower to the other, using royal icing and a no. 1 tube (tip), ensuring that the base of the loop is no less than 1cm (½ in) from the road beneath. Pipe a loop at each end, from the tower to the road. Leave to dry for at least 30 minutes.

~ 2 ~

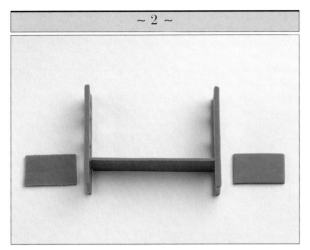

Using tiny amounts of flower paste glue, applied with a cocktail stick (toothpick), glue the bridge pieces together, and leave to dry.

~ 3 ~

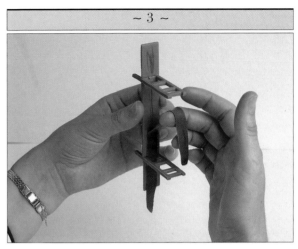

Roll out some dark grey flower paste until 1.5mm (¹⁄₁₆ in) thick. Cut out a strip 1cm (½ in) wide and attach lengths to each bridge for the road, using egg white or gum glue. Leave to dry.

~ 5 ~

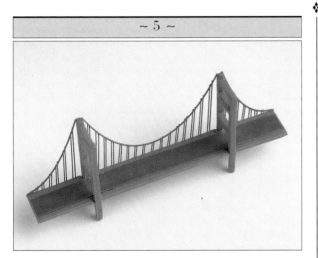

Using a no. 0 tube, pipe in the vertical lines in pairs, with a larger space between each pair. Make sure the lines are vertical and not sloping. Remove excess icing with a damp paintbrush. To finish, pipe a horizontal line across the vertical lines just above the road.

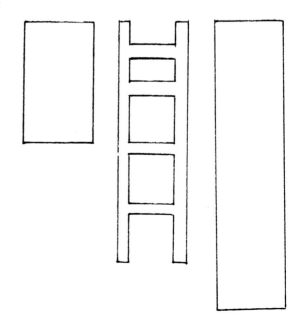

Flower paste bridge pieces

SPORTS CAR *To make an impression of the car on top of the cake, gently press the patchwork cutter into the soft sugarpaste before leaving it to skin over.*

Roll out red, black and light grey mexican paste until 1.5mm (¹⁄₁₆ in) thick. Lightly grease the car cutter and cut out one complete car in each colour, regreasing the cutter each time. Moisten the embossed outline with water. Cut out and fit the pieces.

Surround the car with dark grey mexican paste. Extra pieces of paste can be added to the car to create a 3D effect. Pipe in the inscription with royal icing and a no. 1 piping tube (tip). Over-pipe using a no. 0 tube.

Detail of completed cake side.

Road Bridge Birthday Cake
working drawing
(enlarge to 182% on a
photocopier)

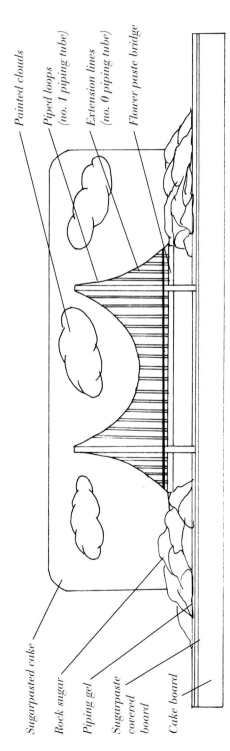

Painted clouds

Piped loops
(no. 1 piping tube)

Extension lines
(no. 0 piping tube)

Flower paste bridge

Sugarpasted cake

Rock sugar

Piping gel

Sugarpaste
covered
board

Cake board

CROCHET WORK BIRTHDAY CAKE

20cm (8 in) round cake, covered with marzipan
(almond paste)
cream and brown sugarpaste
royal icing (without glycerine/glycerol)
selection of liquid and paste food colourings
white vegetable fat (shortening)
flower paste
cornflour dusting bag
egg white or gum glue
soft brown sugar
flower paste flowers and leaves

EQUIPMENT

28cm (11 in) round cake board
embosser (optional)
nos. 0 and 1 piping tubes (tips)
tilting turntable
glass-headed pins
fine paintbrush
butchers' wrap (acetate)
piece of perspex
masking tape
small primrose and leaf cutters
two 6cm (2½ in) patty tins
10cm (4 in) plain round cutter
cocktail stick (toothpick)
tweezers
clay gun (optional)

● Cover the cake with cream-coloured sugar-paste, and impress an inscription on top of the cake, following the instructions on page 8, if desired. Using the working drawing on page 37 as a guide, create a paper template for the side of the cake, cutting 12 equally spaced 'V' shapes along the top edge. Secure the paper template to the cake side and scribe the 'V'

pattern on to the cake. Remove the template, and cut away the cream-coloured sugarpaste below the scribed line.

● Roll out a strip of brown sugarpaste, place the paper pattern on top and cut out. Moisten the cake side and inlay the brown sugarpaste.

● Cover the cake board with brown sugarpaste and emboss, if desired. Pipe a snail's trail around the base of the cake in brown royal icing using a no. 1 piping tube. Leave to skin over for 24 hours.

● Put the cake on a tilting turntable. Secure the paper pattern to the cake side again, this time with the points downwards. Position a glass-headed pin in the cake side just below each point of the paper pattern. Remove the paper pattern. Melt a small amount of white vegetable fat and paint it on to the pins.

● Pipe lines from one pin to the next with royal icing using a no. 0 piping tube. It is not necessary for all the lines to be the same distance from the cake, but it is important that each line touches the next (see step 1 on page 35). Leave to dry for no less than 30 minutes.

● Pipe the vertical lines approximately 5mm (¼ in) apart with cream royal icing using a no. 0 piping tube, from the join formed on the side of the cake by the two colours of sugarpaste to beyond the suspended bridge, ensuring that the lines are vertical and not sloping. Remove the excess royal icing with a damp paintbrush. Do not stop piping on the bridge as the contact of the piping tube with the suspended bridge could cause it to break. (See step 2.) As each pin is approached, carefully remove it.

● Once all the vertical lines are complete, tilt the turntable to the steepest angle possible. Pipe the horizontal lines with royal icing using a no. 0 piping tube, piping the line and turning the

tilting turntable at the same time (this requires much practice). (See step 3.)

Once all the lines are complete, create the crochet pattern by piping two or three lines in alternate squares created by the extension lines, using a no. 0 piping tube. Pipe bulbs along the bottom edge of the crochet work using a no. 0 piping tube.

To make the primrose side decorations, lay a piece of butchers' wrap over the piece of perspex, and attach with masking tape. Roll out some cream-coloured flower paste until 1.5mm (¹⁄₁₆ in) thick, transfer to the perspex and cut out small primroses and leaves (see opposite). Leave to dry, then decorate with cream brush embroidery. Once dry, release from the butchers' wrap and attach to the cake along the top edge of the crochet work using cream-coloured royal icing and a no. 1 piping tube.

The flower basket is made from flower paste, softened and coloured in the usual way. Polish the two patty tins with a clean dry cloth, inside and out. Dust the inside of one and the outside of the other with cornflour.

Roll out some flower paste until 3mm (⅛ in) thick, and cut out a 10cm (4 in) round. Place the flower paste in the patty tin that is dusted inside with cornflour, and smooth into shape. Trim the flower paste level with the top edge of the patty tin, then empty it out of the tin and transfer it to the outside of the other patty tin.

Use the side of a cocktail stick to mark horizontal lines around the outside of the basket. Using tweezers, pinch vertical 'struts' between the horizontal lines (see step 1 on page 36). Remove the paste from the patty tin, redust the outside of the tin, then replace the flower paste and allow to dry overnight.

Create the handle by using a clay gun fitted with the small rope disc, or by rolling out two long sausages of flower paste 1.5mm (¹⁄₁₆ in) wide and twisting them together. Bend the handle into shape, ensuring that it is wide enough, then leave to dry overnight.

To complete the basket, create another rope. Moisten the top edge of the basket with egg white or gum glue, and attach the rope to the top edge of the basket. Press down gently to cover the rough top edge of the basket. Moisten the ends of the handle with egg white or gum glue, and press them into the rope around the top edge of the basket. Support the handle in position with small bottles or other items, and allow to dry. (See step 2 on page 36). Roll out two small sausages of flower paste. Fold the sausages in half and twist. Moisten either side of the handle ends with egg white or gum glue, and wrap a twisted sausage of flower paste around each one, ensuring that the ends of the twisted sausages are inside the basket.

Moisten the inside of the dried basket with egg white or gum glue, and fill with sugarpaste. Moisten the top of the sugarpaste with egg white or gum glue. Colour some soft brown sugar with dark brown food colouring to create a soil effect, and spread over the sugarpaste. Dip the wires of the chosen flowers in egg white or gum glue and insert into the sugarpaste. Secure the basket on the cake with royal icing. Pipe over the embossed inscription following the instructions on page 8, if desired.

~ 1 ~

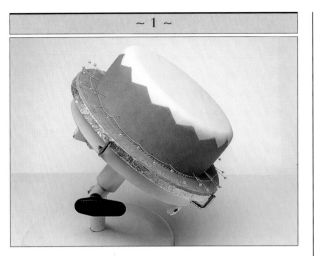

PIPED BRIDGE AND CROCHET WORK *Pipe lines from one pin to the next. It is not necessary for all the lines to be the same distance from the cake, but it is important that each line touches the next. Leave to dry for at least 30 minutes.*

~ 2 ~

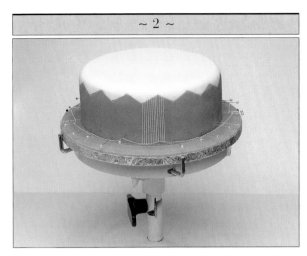

Pipe lines approximately 5mm (¼ in) apart from the join in the sugarpaste to just beyond the suspended bridge. Do not stop on the bridge as it could break; remove excess icing with a damp brush. Carefully remove the pins as you come to them.

~ 3 ~

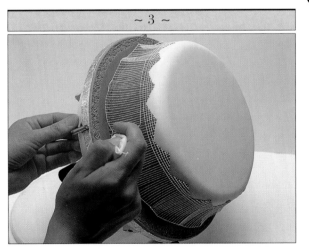

Tilt the turntable to its steepest angle. Pipe in the horizontal lines, turning the cake as you go. Complete the crochet pattern by piping two or three lines in alternate squares (see detail picture on page 36).

~ ❖ ~

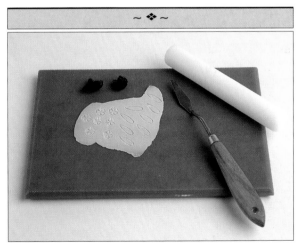

CUT-OUT PRIMROSES *Roll out some cream-coloured flower paste until 1.5mm (¹⁄₁₆ in) thick, and cut out small primroses and leaves. Leave to dry, then decorate with cream brush embroidery. Leave to dry.*

~ 1 ~

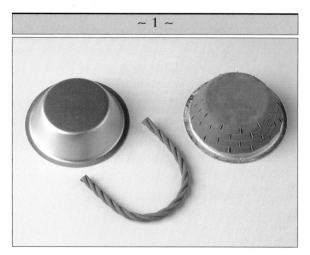

FLOWER BASKET *Use a cocktail stick (toothpick) to mark horizontal lines around the basket. Pinch with tweezers to create vertical struts. The handle is made using a clay gun fitted with the small rope disc, or by twisting together two long sausages (1.5mm/1/16 in wide) of flower paste.*

~ 2 ~

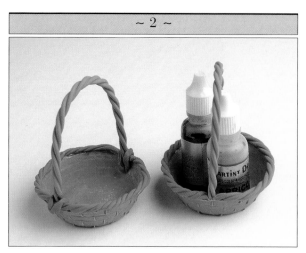

Moisten the handle ends with egg white or gum glue, and press into the rope around the top edge of the basket. Support the handle with small bottles. Moisten the dry handle ends on either side with egg white or glue and wrap a twisted sausage of paste around each end. Leave to dry.

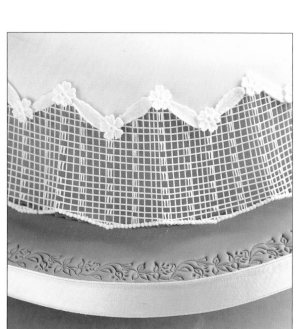

Detail of cake side crochet work

Detail of flower basket and flowers

Crochet Work Birthday Cake
working drawing
(enlarge to 164% on a
photocopier)

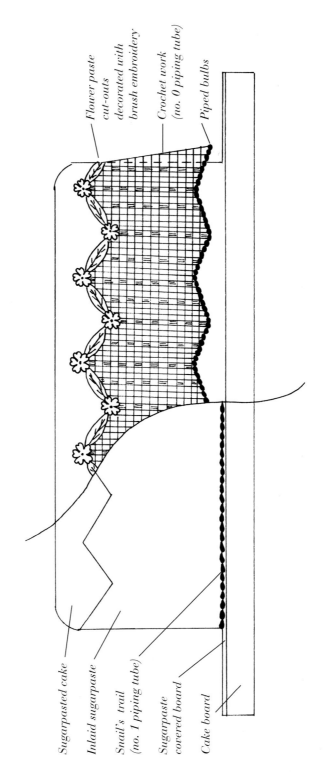

Flower paste
cut-outs
decorated with
brush embroidery

Crochet work
(no. 0 piping tube)

Piped bulbs

Sugarpasted cake

Inlaid sugarpaste

Snail's trail
(no. 1 piping tube)

Sugarpaste
covered board

Cake board

WEDDING ANNIVERSARY CAKE

20cm (8 in) petal cake, covered with marzipan
(almond paste)
sugarpaste
royal icing (without glycerine/glycerol)
white vegetable fat (shortening)
flower paste
cornflour dusting bag
egg white or gum glue

EQUIPMENT

28cm (11 in) petal cake board
rose and leaf embossers (optional)
5mm (¼ in) embroidered satin ribbon
no. 0 piping tube (tip)
25cm (10 in) petal cake tin
cream horn tin
fine paintbrush
miniature wired sugar flowers
florists' tape
cocktail stick (toothpick)

● Cover the cake with sugarpaste, impress the top with an inscription (see page 8), if desired, and leave for at least 7 days before proceeding.

● Cover the cake board with sugarpaste and emboss the edge if desired. Attach 5mm (¼ in) ribbon around the base of the cake. Scribe a line around the cake at the required depth for the extension work. Pressure pipe embroidery on the side of the cake with coloured royal icing and a no. 0 piping tube.

● Place a block inside the cake tin and position the cake on the block, ensuring that the base of the cake is approximately 3mm (⅛ in) lower than the rim of the cake tin, and that the cake is in the centre of the tin. Grease the rim of the tin with white vegetable fat.

● Using royal icing and a no. 0 piping tube, pipe extension lines from the cake to the cake tin rim (see step 1 on page 40). Pipe the lines as closely together as possible without touching. If they touch, remove them. If a line has to be removed, re-grease the cake tin rim at that point before re-piping.

● Pressure pipe hearts along the top edge of the extension lines with a no. 0 piping tube. Pipe bulbs or dots around the base of the extension work, ensuring they touch the extension lines (see step 2). Leave to dry.

● Carefully lift the cake up off the cake tin in one straight movement. Do not tilt the cake or the extension lines will break. Secure the cake on the covered cake board with royal icing.

● For the bouquet of flowers, soften the flower paste in the usual way, colouring it if desired. Polish the outside of the cream horn tin with a clean dry cloth, then dust with cornflour. Roll out the flower paste until 1.5mm (¹⁄₁₆ in) thick. Make a template from the bouquet 'wrapper' outline on page 40, and use it to cut out a piece of the rolled-out paste.

● Wrap the flower paste around the cream horn tin. Paint a line of egg white or gum glue along the edge and secure. Pinch the base of the point with thumb and index finger. Remove the flower paste from the cream horn tin. Re-dust the tin and replace the moulded flower paste. Leave to dry for 12 hours. Dust or paint the dried flower paste if desired. (See step 1 on page 41.)

● Tape the miniature wired flowers into a bunch. Roll a piece of flower paste into a cone, and secure it in the base of the dried cone with egg white or gum glue. Paint a small amount of egg white or gum glue on the base of the wire spray and push it into the flower paste in the

~ 1 ~

EXTENSION WORK *Pipe lines from the scribed line on the cake side to the rim of the tin, keeping the lines as close together as possible without touching.*

~ 2 ~

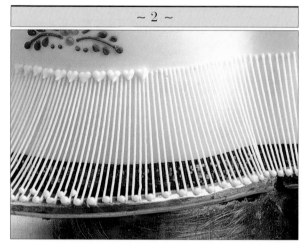

Pressure pipe hearts along the top edge of the extension lines, keeping them as evenly sized as possible. Pipe bulbs or dots around the base of the extension work, making sure they touch the ends of the lines.

cone. Attach to the cake with a small amount of royal icing. (See step 2.)

● Using the photograph on page 41 as a guide, model a champagne bottle from dark green flower paste, and leave to dry. Roll out a piece of white flower paste and cut out a label. Attach to the dried bottle with egg white or gum glue. Make the top out of beige flower paste and attach it to the champagne bottle. Attach to the cake with a small amount of royal icing. Pipe over the inscription as described on page 8, if desired.

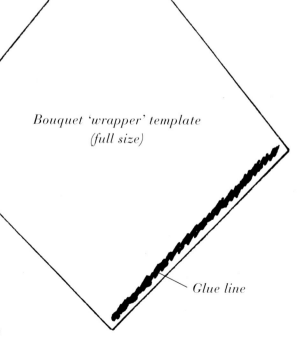

*Bouquet 'wrapper' template
(full size)*

Glue line

~ 1 ~

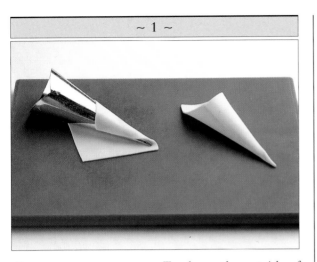

BOUQUET OF FLOWERS To shape the outside of the bouquet, wrap the piece of flower paste around a cream horn tin dusted with cornflour. Paint along the edge with egg white or gum glue to secure. The 'wrapper' can be painted or dusted with colour after drying, if desired.

~ 2 ~

Shape a small piece of flower paste into a cone and push it gently into the dried 'wrapper'. Tape the wires of the miniature roses together with florists' tape. Brush the end with egg white or gum glue and insert it gently into the flower paste cone.

~ ❖ ~

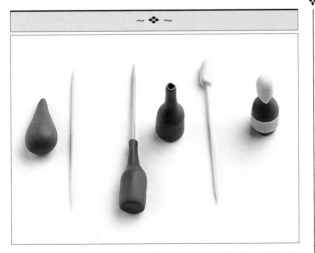

CHAMPAGNE BOTTLE Start with a bulb of dark green flower paste, insert a cocktail stick (toothpick) into the narrow end, and mould it into a bottle shape. The top is made from a small piece of beige flower paste. Add a white flower paste label.

~ ❖ ~

Detail of cake side.

Wedding Anniversary Cake
working drawing
(enlarge to 130% on a
photocopier)

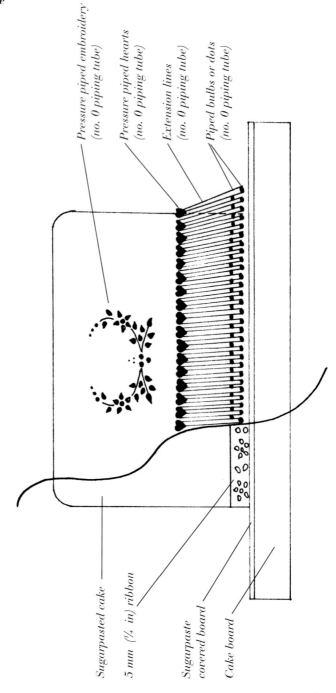

Pressure piped embroidery
(no. 0 piping tube)

Pressure piped hearts
(no. 0 piping tube)

Extension lines
(no. 0 piping tube)

Piped bulbs or dots
(no. 0 piping tube)

Sugarpasted cake

5 mm (¼ in) ribbon

Sugarpaste
covered board

Cake board

CROSS STITCH BIRTHDAY CAKE

20cm (8 in) round cake, coated with marzipan
(almond paste)
royal icing (without glycerine/glycerol)
selection of liquid food colourings

E Q U I P M E N T

28cm (11 in) round cake board
butchers' wrap (acetate)
30cm (12 in) square of perspex
masking tape
nos. 0 and 1 piping tubes (tips)
fine paintbrush
small pieces of sponge
tweezers

● Coat the cake with royal icing and, once dry, coat the board with royal icing. Leave to dry.

● Make tracings of the scissors on page 49, and the cake side piece on page 50. Following the instructions on page 7, if necessary, make run-out sugar scissors (double-sided) and eighteen double-sided run-out sugar side pieces (plus some spares). (The side piece outline is for a cake with a depth of 7.5cm/3 in; amend the template on page 50 to fit your cake, if necessary.)

● Attach the run-out pieces to the side of the cake (evenly spaced) with a no. 1 piping tube, as shown on page 44. Leave to dry for about 24 hours.

● Using the working drawing on page 49 as a guide, make a paper pattern (actual size) of the top lattice rose design. Colour it as required. (The pattern needs to be in colour as it will not be possible to see the symbols once the lattice has been piped.) Try to use colours which contrast.

● Attach the coloured pattern to the piece of perspex or a piece of glass with masking tape (a cake board is not suitable as most are slightly warped). Cover the pattern with a piece of butchers' wrap and attach to the perspex with masking tape. Using royal icing and a no. 0 piping tube, pipe the vertical lines of the lattice, then the horizontal lines.

● Create the picture by piping dots with a no. 0 piping tube into the squares created by the lattice lines in the appropriate colours. If shades of one colour are required, start with the darkest shade first, then add an equal quantity of white royal icing to make a lighter shade.

● Pipe two lines around the lattice, as in the drawing, piping one line on the edge of the lattice. Flood the area between the two lines with run sugar, then place under an angled desk lamp to dry the surface of the run sugar quickly and so keep the sheen. Leave for 30 minutes, then transfer to a warm environment to dry completely. (See page 44.)

● Measure the gap between each run-out piece attached to the cake side. Make coloured patterns from the A–Z cross-stitch designs on pages 46-48, amending the sizes to fit from one run-out side piece to the next. Attach the patterns to the perspex or glass with masking tape. Cover the patterns with butchers' wrap and attach to the perspex with masking tape.

● Using royal icing and a no. 0 piping tube, pipe the lattices, starting with the vertical lines, then piping the horizontal. Create the A–Z pictures by piping dots with a no. 0 piping tube into the squares created by the lattice lines in the appropriate colours. Using a no. 0 piping tube, pipe small bulbs around the edge of each lattice to secure, ensuring that the bulbs touch each other. Leave to dry.

● Make a paper pattern of the scalloped circle on page 49, and place it centrally on top of the cake. Pipe around the outline with a no. 0 piping tube. Remove the paper pattern carefully without breaking the piped line.

● Attach the run-out scissors to the cake top with royal icing, ensuring that part of the scissors is within the piped scalloped circle.

● Place five small pieces of sponge (1.5cm/¾ in square) within the piped scalloped circle. Release the lattice top piece from the butchers' wrap, and place it on top of the small pieces of sponge, ensuring that the lattice is centrally placed within the piped scalloped circle, and that the small pieces of sponge protrude beyond the piped lattice.

● Using royal icing and a no. 0 piping tube, touch the lattice and pipe a line at an angle of 45° until the line touches the piped scalloped circle. Pipe beyond the circle and remove the excess line with a damp paintbrush. Do not tilt the cake but let the line sag gently. Continue to pipe the lines around the lattice, keeping them as close together as possible without touching. As each piece of sponge is approached, remove it carefully with tweezers. (See page 46.)

● Having piped all the way round, pipe the opposite way, i.e. anti-clockwise if the first set of lines was piped clockwise. Pipe the finishing touches to the run sugar embroidery frame using a no. 1 piping tube. Pipe a needle and thread on to the top of the cake with a no. 0 piping tube. Using royal icing and a no. 1 piping tube, attach the A–Z lattices to the double-sided run-outs previously attached to the cake side, removing any excess royal icing with a fine paintbrush (see page 46). Pipe bulbs around the top outside edge of the cake with a no. 1 piping tube.

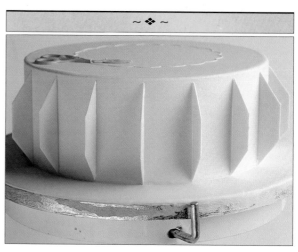

RUN-OUT SUGAR SIDE PIECES Using royal icing and a no. 1 piping tube (tip), attach the run-out sugar side pieces, spacing them evenly all around the cake. Remove any excess icing with a damp paintbrush.

LATTICE TOP PIECE After piping the lattice, pipe in the coloured rose design, following the colour pattern beneath the butchers' wrap. The circular frame is made by flooding the area between two piped lines with run sugar.

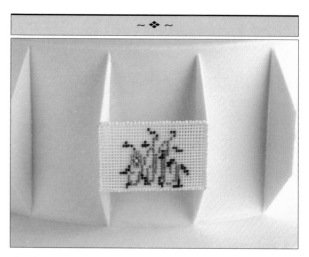

TOP EXTENSION WORK *Pipe lines from the edge of the top lattice piece, at an angle of 45°, to the piped scalloped circle, allowing the lines to sag a little, and removing the pieces of sponge as you come to them.*

A–Z LATTICES *Use a no. 1 piping tube (tip) to attach the 'embroidered' lattice side pieces, positioning them as shown in the working drawing on page 50. Remove excess icing with a fine paintbrush to keep the finish neat.*

A-Z lattices

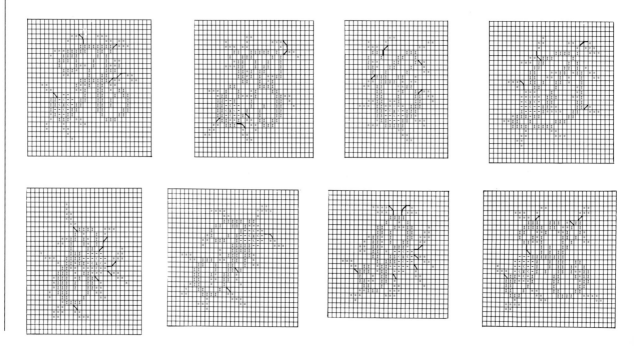

A-Z lattices

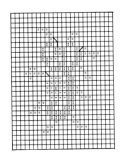
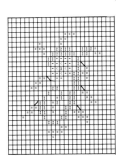
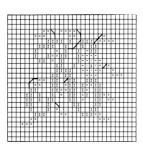
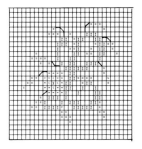

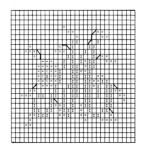
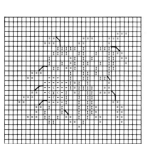
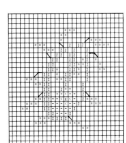
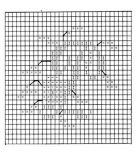

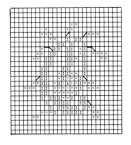
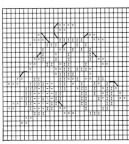

KEY TO COLOURS

X	*Yellow*
–	*Light pink*
<	*Dark pink*
=	*Green*
Z	*Dark tan*

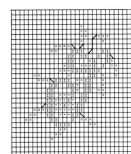
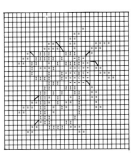

A-Z lattices

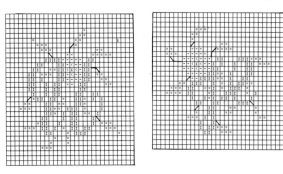
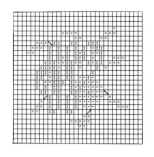
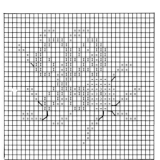

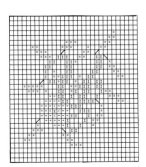
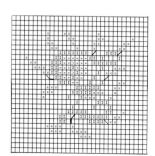
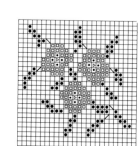
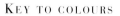

KEY TO COLOURS

△ *Yellow*

▢ *Light pink*

◉ *Dark pink*

● *Green*

Above: the 27th square is for a personal design or use the flower pattern above.

Left: detail of cake side

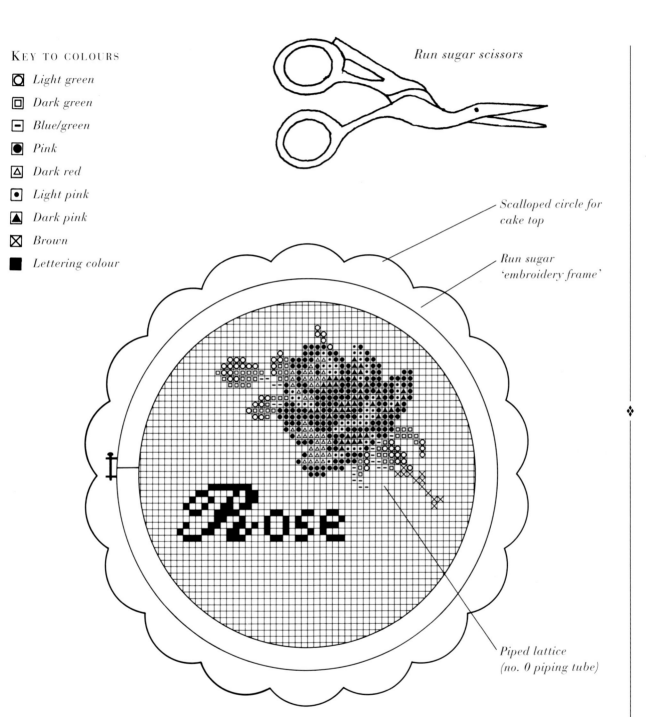

KEY TO COLOURS

- ◨ Light green
- ▣ Dark green
- ⊟ Blue/green
- ◉ Pink
- △ Dark red
- ⊡ Light pink
- ▲ Dark pink
- ⊠ Brown
- ■ Lettering colour

Run sugar scissors

Scalloped circle for cake top

Run sugar 'embroidery frame'

Piped lattice (no. 0 piping tube)

Cross stitch pattern for top lattice piece

Cross Stitch Birthday Cake working drawing
(enlarge to 173% on a photocopier)

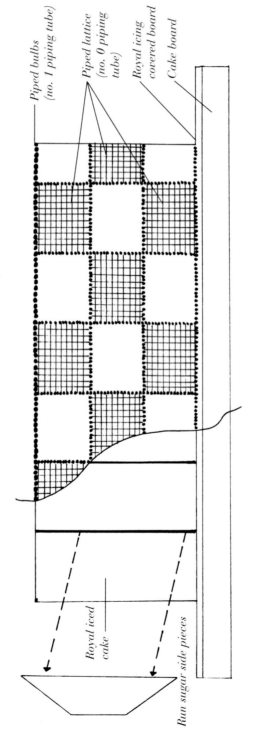

Piped bulbs (no. 1 piping tube)

Piped lattice (no. 0 piping tube)

Royal icing covered board

Cake board

Royal iced cake

Run sugar side pieces

Run sugar side piece (full size)

THREE-TIER WEDDING CAKE

15cm (6 in) oval cake with depth of 6cm
(2½ in) before covering with marzipan
(almond paste)
20cm (8 in) oval cake with depth of 7.5cm
(3 in) before covering with marzipan
(almond paste)
25cm (10 in) oval cake with depth of 8.5cm
(3½ in) before covering with marzipan
(almond paste)
royal icing (without glycerine/glycerol)
selection of liquid food colourings
yellow dusting powder (petal dust/blossom tint)

E Q U I P M E N T

three chamfered cake boards (20cm/8 in on
25cm/10 in, 25cm /10 in on 30cm/12 in, and
30cm/12 in on 36cm/14 in), see page 8
butchers' wrap (acetate)
30cm (12 in) square of perspex
masking tape
nos. 0, 1 and 2 piping tubes (tips)
fine paintbrush
flat-headed brush for dusting
cake inverter stand

● Prepare the chamfered cake boards (see page 8). Coat the cakes and chamfered boards with white royal icing.

● Make templates of the collar sections from the outlines on page 69. Following the instructions on page 7, if necessary, pipe and flood run-out sugar collars in yellow royal icing using a no. 0 piping tube. Make templates for the run sugar upright pieces, amending the sizes, if necessary, so that they will fit together with the collar pieces. Pipe the outlines and flood with yellow royal icing on one side and white royal icing on the other, using a no. 0 piping tube (see page 7).

● Using the outlines on page 52, pipe and flood run-out bells in white royal icing using a no. 0 piping tube, following the flooding order shown on page 54.

● Using the outlines on page 55, pipe and flood the double-sided run-out bears (see page 7). Once the bride and groom bears are dry, pipe the outline of the small oval base (see template on page 56) on to a piece of butchers' wrap attached to a piece of perspex, using a no. 0 piping tube. Pipe a fat line in the centre of the oval and stand the bride and groom in it. Support the bears in position with some small boxes until the icing is dry (see page 54). Flood the oval with run sugar. Once the run sugar has dried, pipe the groom's feet. Finish the edge of the run sugar oval by piping a small scalloped line with white royal icing and a no. 0 piping tube. Repeat with the other run-out bears and ovals.

● Make a scalloped paper template for each of the cake sides (twelve scallops each), and secure to the cakes with tape. Pipe the outline of the template on to the cake sides with a no. 0 piping tube. Pipe a scalloped pattern on to each cake board to match the cake side. Attach the run-out collars to the tops of the cakes, and fill in any gaps. Leave to dry for 1 hour. Pipe a snail's trail around the base of each cake with a no. 1 piping tube. Dust the cake sides with yellow dusting powder as shown on page 54.

● Pipe interlocked initials on to the cake sides in white royal icing with a no. 1 piping tube, then over-pipe with purple royal icing using a no. 0 piping tube. Attach the run-out bells to the cakes with royal icing. Pressure pipe flowers and leaves on to the bells with a no. 0 tube.

● Turn the cake(s) upside-down. To do this safely, place the cake on the palm of your left hand, place the cake inverter stand on top of the cake, hold the central column of the stand with your right hand, ensuring your thumb is pointing to the floor, and turn the cake.

● Pipe the extension lines from the cake side to the edge of the collar, at an angle of approximately 45° using white royal icing and a no. 0 piping tube. The lines will sag gently because of gravity; this helps to create the desired effect. The lines should be as close together as possible without touching. (See step 1 on page 56.)

● Once the lines have been piped all the way round the cake, pipe lines in the other direction, i.e. anti-clockwise if the first set of lines was piped clockwise around the cake. Finish off the scalloped edge on the cake side by piping graduated lines in white royal icing. For the first row, pipe a scalloped line around the cake with a no. 2 piping tube, over-pipe with a no. 1 piping tube, then over-pipe with a no. 0 piping tube. For the second row, which should be as close as possible to the first row without touching it, pipe a scalloped line around the cake with a no. 1 piping tube, then over-pipe the line with a no. 0 piping tube. For the third row, which should be as close as possible to the second row without touching it, pipe a scalloped line around the cake with a no. 0 piping tube. (See the detail photograph on page 54 for guidance.)

● Turn the cake(s) the right way up. Attach the upright double-sided run-out pieces to the cake top. Complete the extension work by piping lines from the upright double-sided pieces to the collar edge, and then from the cake side to the piped scalloped line on the chamfered cake board. (See step 2 on page 56.)

● Finish the edges of the run-out collars and run-out top pieces by piping bulbs with white royal icing and a no. 0 piping tube. Pipe graduated line work on the cake side and chamfered cake board using nos. 0, 1 and 2 piping tubes, as described above. Pressure pipe flowers and leaves (no. 0 piping tube) on the board. Pipe grass and flowers on the cake top.

Run sugar bells

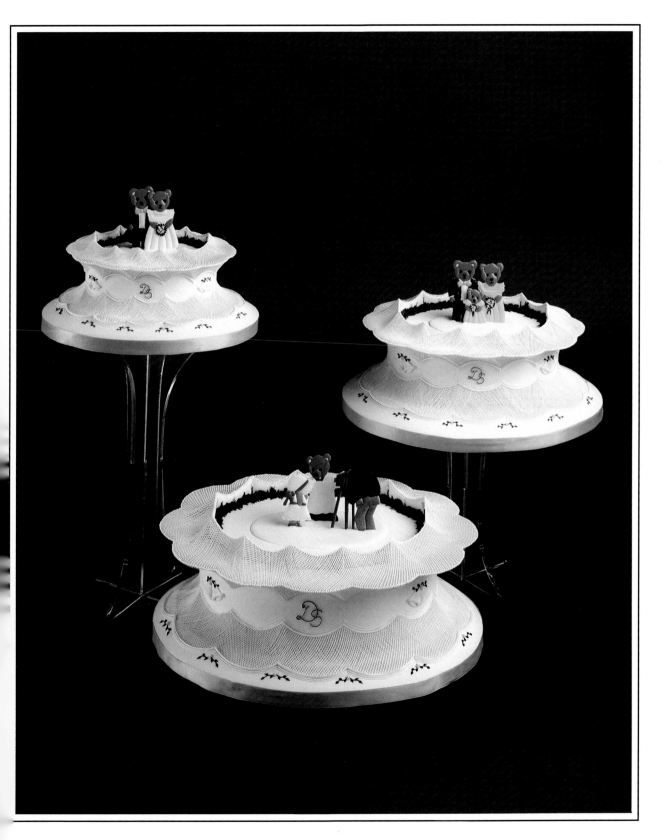

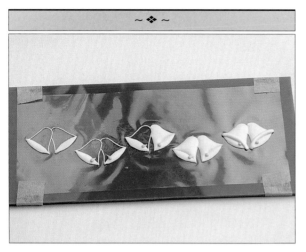

RUN-OUT BELLS *After piping the outlines, flood the different areas of the bells in the order shown. Use a fine paintbrush to pull the icing into every corner. Pipe the clapper in yellow royal icing of normal piping consistency.*

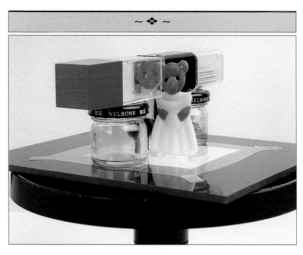

BEARS *Pipe a fat line of royal icing and stand the bride and groom bears on it. Support the bears in position with small boxes, jars or other items until the icing is dry.*

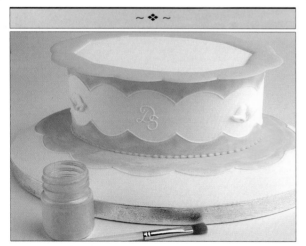

SIDE DUSTING *Dust above and below the piped scalloped lines on the cake sides, and within the scalloped line on the cake boards, with yellow dusting powder (petal dust/blossom tint). Pipe interlocked initials on the cake sides, then attach the run-out bells.*

Detail of top and side of cake

Run sugar bears

~ 1 ~

EXTENSION WORK With the cake upside-down on the cake inverter stand, pipe lines from the scalloped line on the cake side to the edge of the collar, at an angle of approximately 45°. As you pipe the lines, allow them to sag gently.

~ 2 ~

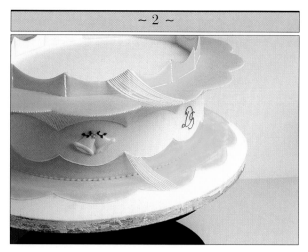

With the cake the right way up, pipe lines from the top of the upright run-out pieces to the edge of the collar, and then from the scalloped line on the cake side to the scalloped line on the board. Pipe first in one direction around the cake, and then in the other, as before.

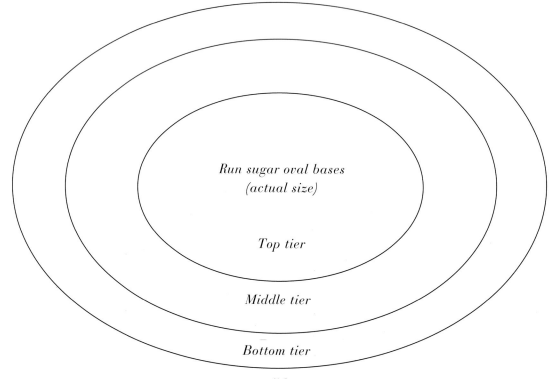

Run sugar oval bases
(actual size)

Top tier

Middle tier

Bottom tier

***Three-tier Wedding Cake
working drawing***
*(enlarge to 195% on a
photocopier)*

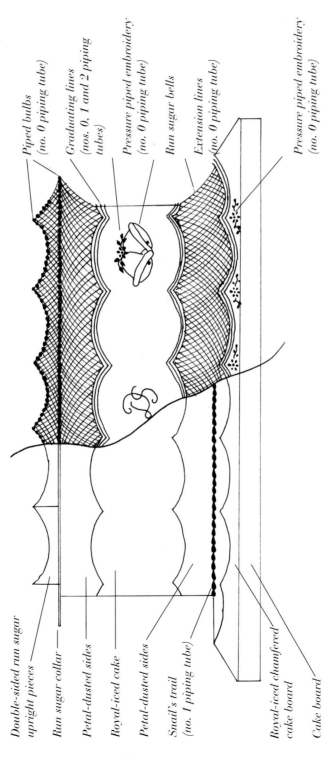

Piped bulbs
(no. 0 piping tube)

Graduating lines
(nos. 0, 1 and 2 piping
tubes)

Pressure piped embroidery
(no. 0 piping tube)

Run sugar bells

Extension lines
(no. 0 piping tube)

Pressure piped embroidery
(no. 0 piping tube)

Double-sided run sugar
upright pieces

Run sugar collar

Petal-dusted sides

Royal-iced cake

Petal-dusted sides

Snail's trail
(no. 1 piping tube)

Royal-iced chamfered
cake board

Cake board

ENGAGEMENT CAKE

royal icing (without glycerine/glycerol)
selection of liquid food colourings
EQUIPMENT
20cm (8 in) oval polystyrene cake dummy with
depth of 6.5cm (2½ in)
28cm (11 in) oval cake board
butchers' wrap (acetate)
piece of perspex
masking tape
nos. 0, 1 and 2 piping tubes (tips)
fine paintbrush
vertical cake holder
cake inverter stand

● Coat the cake dummy with royal icing (using white for the top and pink for the side). Once dry, coat the board with white royal icing and leave to dry.

● Using the working drawing on page 63 as a guide, create a paper pattern for the pink run-out collar that will fit the cake dummy. The collar should protrude 1cm (½ in) beyond and 5mm (¼ in) in from the cake dummy line. (If you need to adjust the pink collar, it will also be necessary to adjust the white collar.)

● Following the instructions on page 7, if necessary, pipe and flood the run sugar collar for the top of the cake dummy in pink royal icing. Leave to dry. Attach to the cake dummy with royal icing and a no. 2 piping tube, removing any excess icing with a fine paintbrush. Leave to dry.

● Create a paper pattern for the oblong side pieces to fit the cake dummy. The full-size pattern on page 62 is for a cake dummy with a depth of 6.5cm (2½ in). Make 18 pink double-sided oblong run-out pieces for the side of the cake dummy, plus some spares. Attach the run sugar pieces vertically to the side of the cake dummy with royal icing and a no. 1 piping tube, removing any excess icing with a fine paintbrush. Leave to dry.

● Make 36 white run sugar squares (1cm/½ in square), plus some spares, for the side of the cake dummy. Leave to dry. Pressure pipe two pink hearts on 18 of the squares, and the initials of the couple on the remaining 18 squares using a no. 0 piping tube.

● Measure the gap between each vertical run-out piece on the cake dummy sides and make double-sided pink run-out pieces to fit horizontally. The easiest way to do this is to make a pattern out of thin cardboard and to use this for the run-out piece; note that each piece will be a different size so you will need to make a different cardboard pattern for each one. Leave to dry. Attach the run-out pieces to the side of the cake dummy at half the cake dummy's depth with royal icing and a no. 1 piping tube, removing any excess icing with a fine paintbrush. Leave to dry.

● Attach the white run sugar squares to the sides of the cake dummy with white royal icing and a no. 0 piping tube, removing any excess icing with a fine paintbrush. Pipe a straight line with a no. 0 piping tube and pink royal icing on the coated cake board, from the base of each vertical run-out side piece to the next (see picture on page 60). Flood this area with pink run sugar, and leave to dry.

● Pipe and flood the second run-out collar for the top of the cake dummy in white royal icing. Leave to dry. Pipe and flood with run sugar using a no. 0 piping tube, the motif for the top of the cake dummy, following the order of flooding shown on page 61. Leave to dry.

● Secure the cake dummy in the vertical cake holder. With white royal icing, pipe a line with a no. 0 piping tube from each corner of the white run sugar squares to the corner of the pink run-out pieces (see step 1 on page 61). Leave to dry. Pipe the extension lines, which should be as close together as possible without touching, ensuring that you are piping with gravity and working at the right position on the vertical cake holder (see step 2).

● Once the side extension lines are completed, remove the cake dummy from the holder, place on a turntable and pipe the bottom extension lines. When these lines are completed, turn the cake dummy upside-down using the following method: place the cake dummy on the palm of your left hand, place the cake inverter stand on top of the cake dummy, hold the central column of the stand with your right hand, ensuring your thumb is pointing to the floor, and turn the cake dummy. Complete the extension lines, then return the cake dummy to the upright position.

● Attach the run-out motif to the cake dummy top and pipe on the inscription. Place approximately 10 small pieces of sponge (1cm/½ in x 5mm/¼ in) on the top of the pink run-out collar. Release the white run sugar collar and place it on top of the small pieces of sponge, ensuring that the collar is central and the small pieces of sponge protrude beyond the collar on the outside edge only.

● Using white royal icing and a no. 0 piping tube, pipe extension lines on the inside edge of the collar, piping from the cake dummy top up to the white collar (see picture on page 61). When complete, pipe the outside extension lines, piping from the edge of the white collar to the edge of the pink collar. As

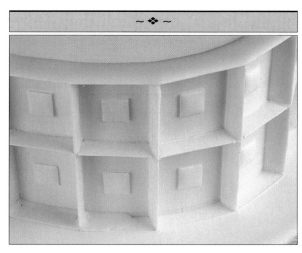

BASE FLOODING After attaching the white run-out squares to the cake side, pipe a line on the cake board from the base of each vertical run-out side piece to the next. Flood the areas within these lines with pink run sugar.

each small piece of sponge is approached, remove it carefully with a pair of tweezers, and continue until the extension lines are complete.

~ 1 ~

SIDE EXTENSION WORK *With the cake dummy in the vertical cake holder, begin by piping a line from each corner of the white run-out squares to the corner formed by the pink run-out pieces.*

~ 2 ~

Pipe vertical lines down to the pink side piece beneath each square. Begin at the end of the left-hand diagonal line just piped, and work from left to right, up the left-hand sloping line, along the edge of the square, and down the right-hand sloping line.

~ ❖ ~

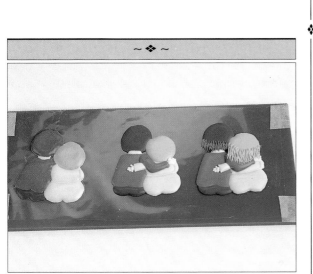

CAKE TOP MOTIF *Using coloured royal icing and a no. 0 piping tube (tip), flood the different areas of the motif in the order shown. Pipe and paint on additional features, such as hair, pullover ribbing and trouser pockets.*

~ ❖ ~

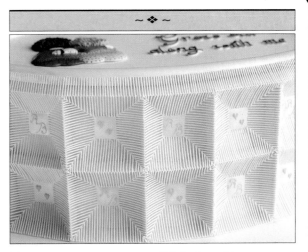

TOP EXTENSION WORK *With the white run-out collar supported on pieces of sponge, first pipe the inside extension lines from the cake surface up to the inner edge of the white collar, then pipe lines from the outer edge of the white collar down to the outer edge of the pink collar.*

***Engagement Cake
working drawing***
*(enlarge to 169% on
a photocopier)*

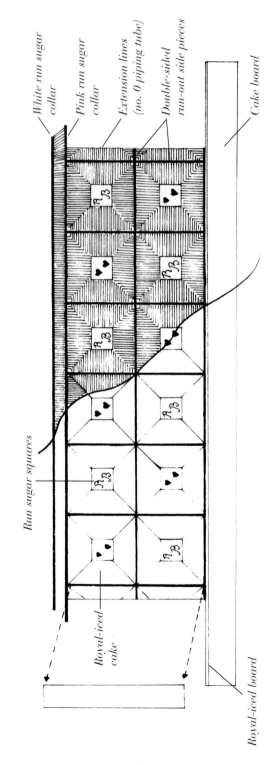

White run sugar collar

Pink run sugar collar

Extension lines
(no. 0 piping tube)

Double-sided
run-out side pieces

Cake board

Run sugar squares

Royal-iced
cake

Royal-iced board

*Run sugar side piece
(full size)*

Engagement Cake top template
(enlarge to 142% on a photocopier)

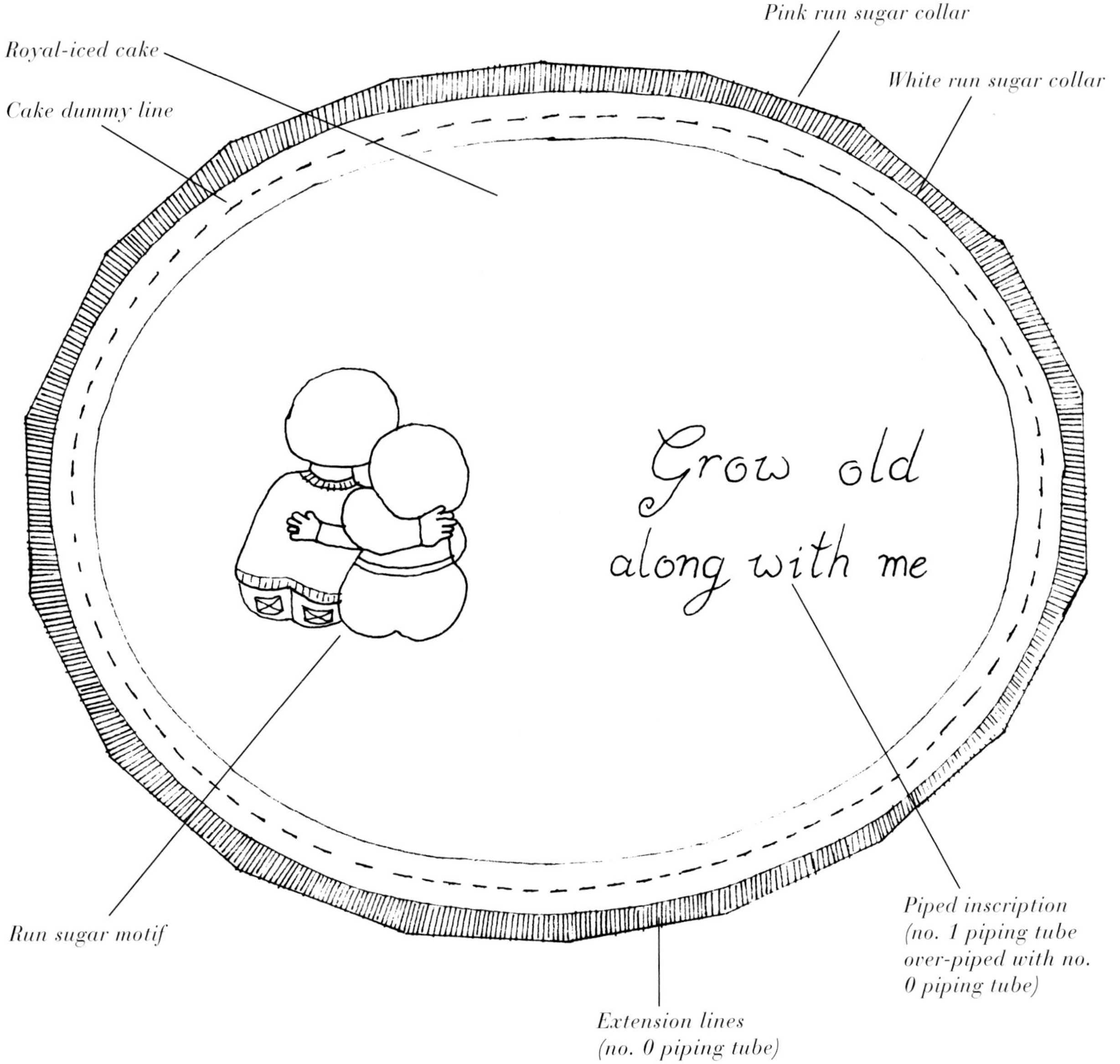

Pink run sugar collar

White run sugar collar

Royal-iced cake

Cake dummy line

Grow old along with me

Run sugar motif

Piped inscription
(no. 1 piping tube over-piped with no. 0 piping tube)

Extension lines
(no. 0 piping tube)

OWL BIRTHDAY CAKE

20cm (8 in) round cake, coated with marzipan
(almond paste)
royal icing (without glycerine/glycerol)

EQUIPMENT

28cm (11 in) round cake board
butchers' wrap (acetate)
piece of perspex
masking tape
nos. 0 and 1 piping tubes (tips)
fine paintbrush
cake tilter

● Coat the cake with royal icing. When dry, coat the board with royal icing. Leave to dry.

● Using the working drawing on page 68, make a tracing of the owl run-out design for the top of the cake. Pipe and flood with run sugar, following the instructions on page 7, if necessary. Make patterns from the triangle templates on pages 67 and 68, amending the side triangle template as necessary to fit your cake after coating. Make 108 run-out triangles for the cake sides and 36 for the top of the cake, plus some spares. Use a no. 0 piping tube and flood the pieces flat.

● Attach the triangles to the side of the cake with royal icing and a no. 1 piping tube, removing any excess icing with a fine paintbrush. Arrange the triangles in three rows, each with 36 evenly spaced triangles (see picture on page 66). Leave to dry for 24 hours.

● Turn the cake upside-down on the cake tilter. To do this, place the cake tilter on top of the cake, hold the cake in the palm of your left hand, place your right hand on top of the tilter and turn the cake over. Adjust the angle of

the cake tilter to approximately 70°. The highest point on the tilter has to be on your left. All lines must be piped with gravity; if the angle is wrong, the lines will be curved (see step 1 on page 66).

● Pipe the extension lines (marked in red on the working drawing on page 67, and shown in gold in step 1) with a no. 0 piping tube. Do not work at the highest or lowest point on the tilter; all work has to be done at the middle point, so turn the cake after completing each section.

● Turn the cake and tilter round so that the highest point is now on your right (see step 2). Pipe the extension lines (shown in green) with a no. 0 piping tube. Turn the cake the right way up and complete the extension work (marked in green/pale blue on the working drawing).

● Attach the 36 flat-topped triangles to the top of the cake with royal icing and a no. 1 piping tube, removing any excess icing with a fine paintbrush, and spacing the triangles evenly around the cake. Leave to dry for 24 hours.

● Attach an inscription to the cake top, if desired, with a no. 0 piping tube, removing excess icing with a fine paintbrush. Pipe a spot of royal icing with a no. 1 piping tube on each triangle around the top of the cake, and attach the top piece, removing excess icing with a fine paintbrush. Tilt the cake and complete the extension work (marked in pink/brown on the working drawing).

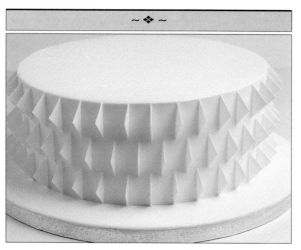

RUN-OUT SIDE TRIANGLES *Arrange the run-out triangles around the cake in three rows, each of 36 triangles, spacing them evenly as shown. Attach them to the cake with royal icing and a no. 1 piping tube (tip), removing excess icing with a paintbrush.*

Detail of cake side

~ 1 ~

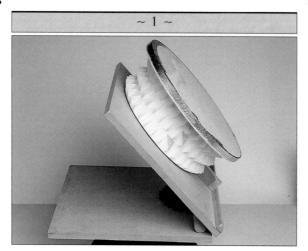

SIDE EXTENSION WORK *With the cake tilted at an angle of approximately 70°, with the highest point on your left, begin piping the first set of extension lines, shown in gold. Work at the middle point of the tilter all the time, turning the cake as you work around it.*

~ 2 ~

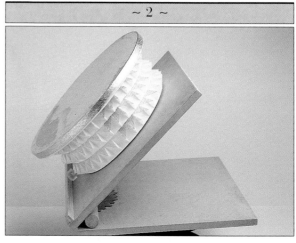

The second set of extension lines, shown in green, are piped with the highest point of the tilter on your right. Again, always work at the middle point of the tilter, turning the cake after piping each section.

Owl Birthday Cake working drawing *(enlarge to 164% on a photocopier)*

Run sugar flat-topped triangles (no. 0 piping tube)

Run sugar triangles (no. 0 piping tube)

Extension work (no. 0 piping tube)

Run sugar top piece

Royal-iced board

Cake board

Run sugar triangle for cake sides (full size)

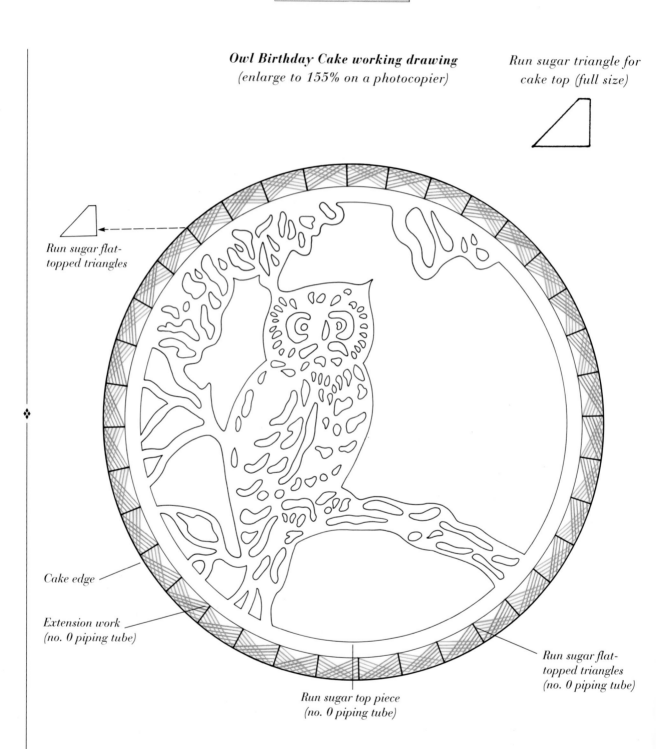

Owl Birthday Cake working drawing
(enlarge to 155% on a photocopier)

*Run sugar triangle for
cake top (full size)*

*Run sugar flat-
topped triangles*

Cake edge

*Extension work
(no. 0 piping tube)*

*Run sugar flat-
topped triangles
(no. 0 piping tube)*

*Run sugar top piece
(no. 0 piping tube)*

TEMPLATES

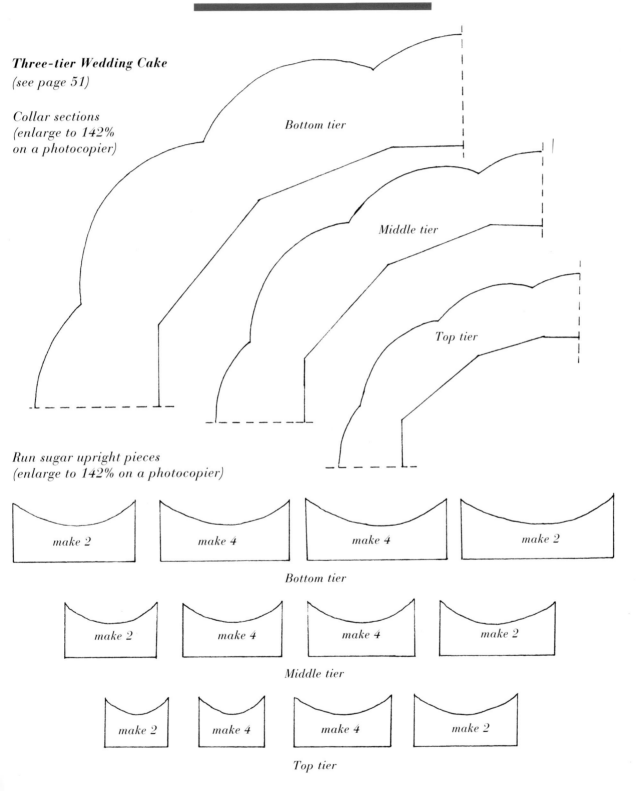

Three-tier Wedding Cake
(see page 51)

*Collar sections
(enlarge to 142%
on a photocopier)*

Bottom tier

Middle tier

Top tier

*Run sugar upright pieces
(enlarge to 142% on a photocopier)*

make 2   *make 4*   *make 4*   *make 2*

Bottom tier

make 2   *make 4*   *make 4*   *make 2*

Middle tier

make 2   *make 4*   *make 4*   *make 2*

Top tier

Useful lower case cross stitch alphabet

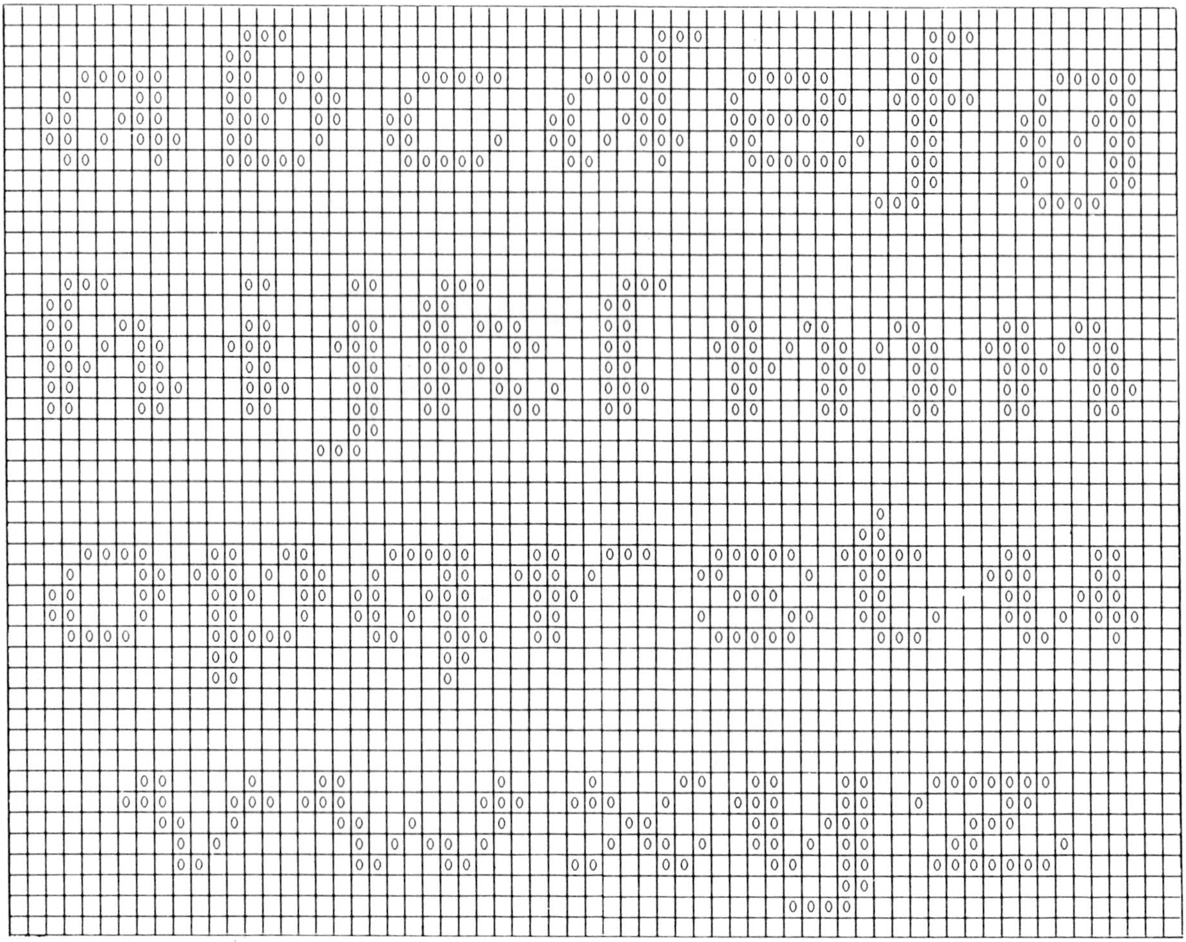

Useful alphabet for piping greetings, see Three-tier Wedding Cake (see page 51) and Engagement Cake (see page 58)

ABCDE
FGHIJKL
MNOPQR
STUVW
XYZ abcde
fghijkl
wxz
mnopqrstuvy

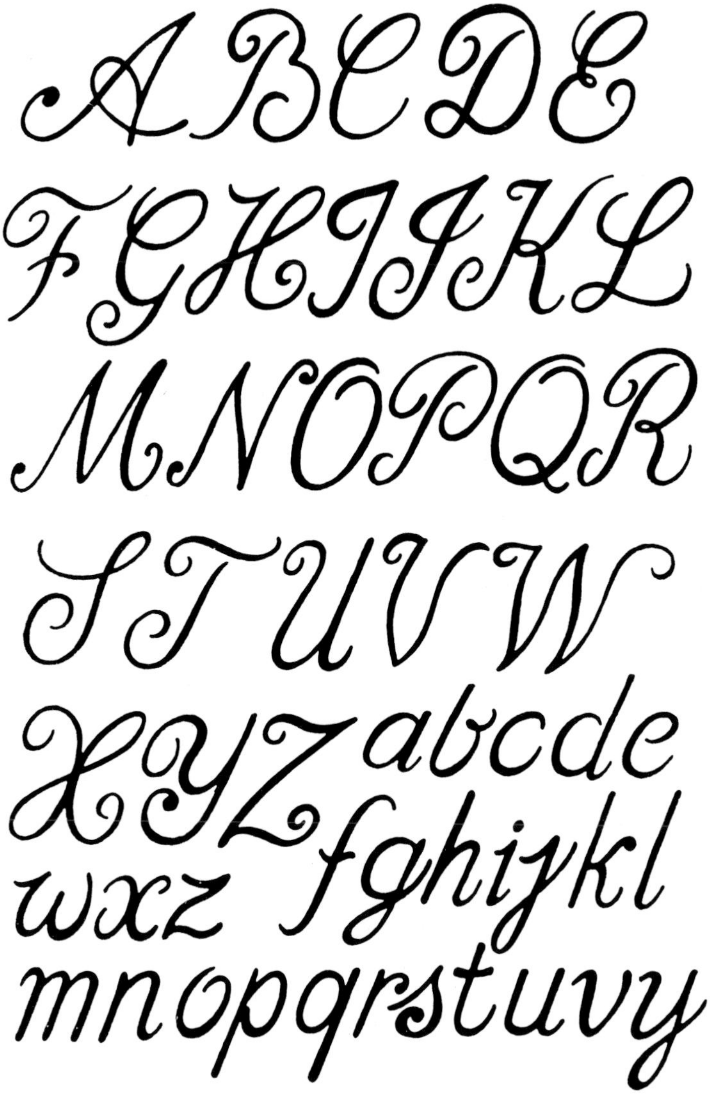

INDEX

FOR FURTHER INFORMATION

Merehurst is the leading publisher of cake decorating books and has an excellent range of titles to suit cake decorators of all levels. Please send for a free catalogue, stating the title of this book:

United Kingdom
Marketing Department
Merehurst Ltd.
Ferry House
51–57 Lacy Road
London SW15 1PR
Tel: 0181 780 1177
Fax: 0181 780 1714

U.S.A./Canada
Foxwood International Ltd.
Suite 426
420 Main Street East, Unit C
Milton, Ontario
L9T 5G3 Canada
Tel: 00 1 905 854 1305
Fax: 00 1 905 854 0978

Australia
J.B. Fairfax Ltd.
80 McLachlan Avenue
Rushcutters Bay
NSW 2011
Tel: (61) 2 361 6366
Fax: (61) 2 360 6262

Other Territories
For further information
contact:
International Sales
Department at United
Kingdom address.